Web-based Career Counseling

A Guide to Internet Resources for Researching a Career and Choosing a Major

Mary E. Ghilani, M.S., NCC

Scranton: University of Scranton Press

Library of Congress Cataloging-in-Publication Data

Ghilani, Mary E., 1958 -
    Web-based career counseling; a guide to Internet resources for researching a career and choosing a major / Mary E. Ghilani.
        p.
    Includes bibliographical references and index.
    ISBN 1-58966-110-9 (pbk.)
    1. Vocational guidance--Computer network resources. 2. Career development--Computer network resources. J. Title.
    HF5382.7.G49 2005
    025.06' 331705--dc22

                                            2005042229

Distribution:

**The University of Scranton Press
Chicago Distribution Center
11030 S. Langley
Chicago, IL 60628**

Contents

Chapter 4

Chapter 5

Chapter 6

Chapter 7

Foreword

This book provides a much-needed resource for the career counseling field. Through the broad topics addressed, this Internet resource guide addresses resources for self-exploration as well as researching both a career and college major. Career counselors in all settings (school, college, private, agency) need to integrate utilization of Web-based resources into both career courses and career counseling interventions.

Contemporary career counseling approaches mandate career counselors utilize Internet resources to facilitate client and student career decision-making. In recent years, the career counseling field has embraced a number of new and innovative counseling models, such as those embracing constructivist, cognitive social learning, and narrative approaches, as well as Krumboltz's "happenstance theory." Whether relying on one of these newer approaches or the "tried and true" theoretical models of trait/factor, Holland, and Super's theoretical constructs, self-assessment and career exploration are consistent elements in the career counseling process.

Ghilani effectively organizes her discussion of web sites around the topics of self-assessment and career explorations. Her discussion of interests, aptitudes, personality traits, and values encourages the reader to examine these self-assessment areas and only utilize assessment results as a guide.

Career exploration Web sites are topically organized and logically congruent with the career counseling process. Further, many specific resources are organized by career cluster area. This helps students and clients keep their options open.

The educational approach provided throughout this guide will keep it current, even if multiple new Web sites on these topics appear. Similar Web sites are examined in each topic area in a holistic career counseling approach. Clearly, Web sites are an integrated part of the career counseling process and not a stand-alone intervention.

Multiple worksheets and guides enhance the educational and counseling process dimension of the book.

Enjoy this guide as it addresses well-known career counseling concepts and constructs with a Web-based content. A sense of practicality and realism for putting the activities and web site explanations and career counseling suggestions into practice is woven throughout *Web-Based Career Counseling*.

LeeAnn Eschbach, Ph.D.
University of Scranton

Acknowledgments

A heartfelt thank you to all those who helped me on my own career decision-making journey.

Special thanks to Dr. LeeAnn Eschbach, Associate Professor and Director of the School Counseling Program at the University of Scranton, for her professional support and guidance; Danielle Richards, Division of Undergraduate Studies Coordinator at the Penn State Berks Campus, for her friendship and editorial comments; Sarah Rodgers, for her administrative support; and finally, to my husband Chuck, for without his patience and helpful suggestions this book would not have become a reality.

Preface

This book is intended to help you make a career decision using the resources of the Internet. The career information, Web sites, and accompanying exercises in this book are designed to actively engage you in the career exploration and investigation process.

Career development is a very personal, individualized process that often continues throughout a person's life. Yet most of us are asked at a very young age to make a decision about a career that will affect the rest of our lives. Without the benefit of experience and information, most of us will have the unfortunate experience of discovering that what we *thought* a career was going to be and what it actually *is* are two entirely different things. That's why occupational research is so important. The career-specific Web sites at the end of this book will not only introduce you to the wealth of career possibilities that exist, but show you how to match your personal characteristics and abilities with a career that will be rewarding and satisfying.

Given today's economic conditions, many of you may have adopted a consumer-oriented approach to choosing a major, college, or career. You, or your parents, may want to know what the economic return will be on your college investment. You may be wondering what kind of job you can expect to find with a major in English, for example; how much you will earn after graduation, and the potential job growth over the next decade. Paramount to that level of sophistication is the need for information. It is unreasonable to expect your academic or career counselor to be knowledgeable about all employment avenues and the nuances of every major, occupation, or career. *Web-Based Career Counseling* will help you access, via the Internet, the most accurate and up-to-date sources of career information available.

The Internet is the latest tool used to explore occupational options. Using the Internet, you can now do more in-depth, extensive research than ever before; do it at home or at school, and subsequently make more thoughtful, informed choices about your career path. As new Web sites are added every day, the Internet is becoming the premier source of occupational and career information.

In whatever capacity you use this book in your own career decision making journey, the author hopes you find this information useful.

CHAPTER 1

How Can Web-Based Career Counseling Help Me?

TRADITIONAL CAREER COUNSELING

The essence of traditional career counseling has always been in the personalized, face-to-face interaction between a student and a trained career or guidance counselor. The counselor asked questions, offered insight, made interpretations, and summarized the results. Students were often asked to complete several pencil and paper inventories or assessments in order to help identify their interests, abilities, values, and personality styles. Counselors used these results, plus interpretation, insight, and counseling skills to help students make sense of the information they gathered, learn more about themselves, and consequently make more informed career choices.

Occupational research typically required students to research occupations by laboriously paging through the *Dictionary of Occupational Titles*, reading career-related books, interviewing professionals, or engaging in some kind of jobshadowing activity at a local industry or business. While all of these activities were extremely useful in identifying potential careers, the problem was that they took so much time.

WEB-BASED CAREER RESOURCES

Thank goodness those days are over! Just as the advancement of the Internet and the World Wide Web has changed the way we interact, conduct business, play, and even shop, so has it changed the way we research careers. Many of the career resources that were traditionally only available in paper format are now available online. As new Web sites are being created, and more and more career counseling professionals, colleges and universities, professional organizations, recruiting agencies, and corporate consultants are putting their services online, there is a wealth of information and services at our fingertips that simply wasn't available five or ten years ago.

We can now research and access career-related information from sources all over the world. With the aid of the Internet, we can perform more in-depth, extensive research than ever before, do it more quickly, access information from home or at school, and subsequently make more thoughtful, informed choices about our career path.

Although nothing can replace the insight and guidance of a well-trained career counselor, the Internet is a powerful tool that can enhance career decision-making. The new problem is that few people have the time to search through the overwhelming number of Web sites in order to find the information they need.

Where do I start? Which sites should I choose? How do I know this site will give me accurate information? *Web-Based Career Counseling* was written to answer these questions by providing a comprehensive resource of free career exploration and occupational Web sites. The career exploration and occupational Web sites in this book have been organized in a way that will hopefully make your search a little easier and your research more efficient.

HOW TO USE THE INTERNET

Before you begin, there are some things you need to remember when using the Internet. One is that the Internet is constantly changing. New sites appear and old sites disappear. Sites also move to new addresses. If you type in an address, or URL (uniform resource locator), for a site that has moved to a different location, you will usually receive a prompt telling you to wait a few seconds while you are automatically forwarded to the new location. Remember to make a note of the new URL or add it to your bookmarks.

You may get a message that the page you are looking for doesn't exist or can no longer be found. In that case, try searching for the site by using one of the many search engines available today. If you place quotation marks around the word, phrase, or title of whatever you are looking for, let's say "Science Careers," the search engine will search for sites containing that specific phrase. If you just simply type in "Science Careers," without quotation marks, then the database will search for *any* web site containing those words or phrase.

The other option is that although the specific page you are looking for may have changed, the homepage may still be active. This is quite common in college and university sites. In this case, log into the college's homepage (e.g., www.college.edu) and then try searching for whatever specific page you are looking for. It is for this reason that many of the Web sites listed in this book have short URL addresses, followed by instructions on how to proceed to a specific page (rather than providing the entire URL address).

Remember to type in the web address *exactly* as it appears. Even one incorrect keystroke can take you to a totally unrelated site. Most of the Web sites in this book will have addresses ending in *.edu, .org, .com, or .gov*. These extensions, or "domains," can help you identify the type of Web site. When organizations register their Web site addresses on the Internet, they are given a Web address, or "domain name," relative to their particular type of organization. Domain names ending in *.edu* are usually reserved for educational organizations (colleges and universities); *.org* for non-profit organizations; *.com* for commercial or personal web sites, and *.gov* for government sites. By noting the domain you can determine, in advance, if a site is free charge (government or university), or if it may charge a fee (commercial site). As the number of web sites on the internet increases you may see some exceptions. For example, an organization may have to use *.com* or *.net* instead of *.org* if the name they wanted is already registered with someone else.

All of the sites listed in this book (with the exception of the *Self-Directed Search*) are free of charge. Some commercial sites offer modified assessment tests at no charge, but then require a fee in order to receive a more detailed report. Unfortunately, there is no guarantee that they will *remain* free of charge in the future, so unless you are willing to pay for extra services, make sure that what you're requesting is still free of charge.

WHERE DO I BEGIN?

So where should you begin? If you're not sure what major or career you might be interested in, then begin with an interest inventory. Complete several inventories or self-assessments. The more information you gather about yourself, the better able you will be to create an accurate picture of who you are.

If you have already completed the self assessment stage, or already know what you're interested in, you can skip to Chapter 9–15 in this book. Find your area of interest, view some Web sites, gather the information, and complete the career sheets in Chapter 7. Then spend some time thinking about the information you have gathered and how it matches with the information you have about yourself. Discuss your results with other people—your friends, your family, your teachers or counselors. And remember that despite what anyone else suggests you do with your life, it is just that—your life! And only *you* can decide which career is right for you.

Best of luck!

CHAPTER 2

"Best Fit" Approach to Choosing a Career

CAREER DEVELOPMENT IS A PROCESS

Deciding on what major to choose or what career to prepare for can be one of the most difficult choices a person has to make. That's because the ultimate goal of choosing a career is to figure out who you are and where you fit in the world of work. Sounds simple enough, but for many of us, that one task may involve a journey that may continue throughout our lifetime. Very few people come into this world knowing exactly what they want to do, get there, and then happily remain in their chosen profession until they retire. Many of us have to search, make mistakes, and go through several bad job experiences before finding the one that is right. Some of us have unforeseen events that happen in our lives and cause us to switch careers or suddenly look in a new direction. Career development, like life, involves growing and developing and adapting the best we can to the events that occur in our lives.

Perhaps the only truism about career development is that you will change your mind at some point along your career. Some research statistics claim that people will change jobs five to seven times, and occupations three to four times, during a work life that may last fifty years or more. That is not necessarily due to lack of direction, but in response to changing times or personal situations. People are complex and dynamic beings. Most of us start out with a one idea of what we want to do, then change and refine that idea throughout our lives. That's why career development is a *process*–not an absolute. Like Bagger Vance said, we "… do the best with what we have to work with."

WHO WE ARE NOW

For most of us that means dealing with who we are at this point in time. If you are in high school, you probably have not accumulated enough work experience to be able to identify what your work values and attitudes are. You may not even realize the full extent of your abilities yet. Some people have talents that, for one reason or other, only surface later in life. Maybe you never knew you could write poetry. You may not have had the opportunity or the inclination to try. Then one day an event like 9/11 happens that touches your emotional core in such a way that you begin to express yourself through writing poetry... and a career in creative writing begins to emerge. Regarding the number of different jobs, careers, and occupations available, you are probably only aware of the ones you have been exposed to in school or through the people you know.

Many professionals, if you were to talk to them about their career path, will say they "stumbled" into their major during college or later in life. This phenomenon has been called the "accident theory" by Bandura (1982) and others. Individuals "accidently" find out about a major they previously never knew existed, through some chance event like going to college, talking to a friend, or sitting in on a guest lecture, etc.

"BEST FIT" APPROACH

There are many theories of career development, both in the literature and in practical use, but none claim to hold a "crystal ball," despite how desperately we hope for one. The truth of the matter is there is no single "best major" for anyone, and in some cases, there may even be several "right" majors.

Given this uncertainty, how can we make the best decision about a work future many years from now? A practical approach to career decision-making that I have used over the years involves finding a career whose characteristics best match, or "fit" who you are. Hence, the "best fit" approach.

Just as people are made up of more than one attribute, so are occupations. A good occupational match is made when the essential factors that make up an individual match, or are at least compatible with, the dominant attributes of a job or career. Think of all the skills that are involved in being a receptionist in a medical office. In order to be successful you would want a person who a) likes people (interests); b) takes pleasure from being helpful and being part of a larger team (values); c) is energized by a fast-paced, often noisy or crowded, and sometimes unpredictable working environment (personality style); and d) has good verbal communication skills, organizational ability, and computer or office technology skills (aptitude). Good receptionists are not only people-oriented, but possess good clerical, computer, and organizational skills as well. The point is that you have to look at *all* of the factors that make up a job and see how well they fit with *all* of the factors that make up a person, not just one. Just because someone enjoys "being with people" doesn't necessarily mean they'd make a good medical receptionist. If that particular individual also happens to be extremely verbal, creative, and prefers to deal with situations as they arise, rather than following an established routine, then that medical office is probably going to end up in chaos. This particular individual might be better suited in a public relations, marketing, or fund-raising career where there is more personal flexibility and the opportunity to exercise creativity and spontaneity.

HOW TO MAKE GOOD CHOICES

The problem is that the career decision-making process generally takes a long time. Some work experience is needed to be able to know if you are someone who is better suited working in an environment where you need periods of quiet in order to complete projects, or thrive off the energy of being "part of a team." Despite the rhetoric that it's "okay to be undecided" in high school or college, our educational system is not really set up in that fashion. Most of you need to have some idea of what your career direction is *before* you enter high school in order to take the appropriate high school courses that will prepare you for entry and success in college.

So what should you do? Perhaps the safest way is to hedge your bets and prepare yourself for the route that will give provide you with the most options. That means taking as many math, science and English classes as possible. That way, you will be prepared for both a science or a non-science major, whenever you're finally ready to make that decision. Most students don't want to hear this, but it is probably the single best piece of academic advice you can receive.

Whatever your situation, exploring who you are and comparing those traits or factors with all of the aspects of an occupation (or of several occupations) will go a long way in helping you to make a better, more informed decision about your future.

CHAPTER 3

Introduction to Self-Assessment

KNOWING WHO YOU ARE

The first step in the choosing the right career is knowing who you are. Self-assessment is the process of exploring and identifying your interests, values, motivations, tendencies, and personality traits. These factors are all critical in coming up with a good occupational match. That's why most career counseling approaches begin by asking you to identify your interests. Identifying your interests is a good place to start, because doing what you like is going to make you happier in the long run.

Abilities (what am I good at, what skills or talents do I possess?) are important in helping you *reach* your career goal. Many students begin college in an academically challenging major like pre-med or engineering with high hopes and aspirations. Unfortunately, some do not fully realize the amount of academic preparation needed to succeed in a rigorous major at the college level. They begin college with much the same way they approached high school. Then they fail their first calculus or chemistry exam, and their second one, and eventually come to the painful realization that they may have to modify their career goals and find another direction. This experience can be extremely traumatic. For this reason, it's wise to take the time to thoroughly understand the requirements of your major, and make an honest assessment of your strengths and weaknesses. That being said, only you can decide what you can succeed at. So go ahead and give it your best shot—but have a backup plan, just in case.

KNOW YOUR OPTIONS

Luckily, most majors have similar or related jobs that can be just as satisfying and rewarding. An example of this is that if you can't be a neurosurgeon, but still enjoy medicine and helping others, there are plenty of other related health care careers such as nursing, radiology, or medical technology. Or you could become a medical counselor or social worker, or other health professional that works with or for the neurosurgeon.

The key is to be able to identify those particular aspects of a profession that interest you. Once you've identified those key factors, you might find they are common to several different professions. Now you've broadened your career options and avoided the common pitfall of being locked into only one career option.

Another problem is that sometimes we tend to be swept up by the fame, prestige, or romance of high profile professions that we forget to look at *all* of the aspects of that career. No matter how glamorous a job appears, there are always negative aspects. Usually a high level of profile or fame are accompanied by an equally high level of stress, pressure, demand on one's personal time, and the very public consequences of making a mistake. In the case of the ER surgeon, you may only be seeing what television wants you to see—fame, wealth, respect, or the quest to save lives. But what you don't see and what you'll have to live with every day in that career are long, grueling hours, the hospital bureaucracy, moments of extreme stress, threats of lawsuit, and the possibility of losing a patient. So know who you are, what you can and cannot handle, and be aware of the reasons behind the choices you make.

THE VALUE OF KNOWING YOUR ABILITIES, VALUES, AND PERSONALITY STYLE

Employers will generally be more interested in your abilities rather than your values. Employers want people who can produce results for their company or organization. You, however, may be more motivated from the personal satisfaction you receive from a job. Using the above example, you may have the interest and ability to be a physician, but may feel compelled to use those skills to help inner city children, or in third world countries where good health care is rare. This altruistic part of the job is called a *value*, and will eventually make a difference in what type of job you choose within a field, and how happy you will be as a result. Being able to identify and prioritize your work values will help you make a better choice of work environments and increase the likelihood that you will find a career that makes getting up in the morning to go to work a pleasure.

When you begin researching careers, compare the results of your self-assessment to the job description. Is there a match? How close or how distant is the match, and how willing are you to put up with the negatives? Ask yourself if this job will allow you to fully use your abilities, maintain your interest, feel fulfilled, not compromise your ideals, allow you to reach your goals, and live the type of life you have always dreamed about.

Personality style involves how well-suited you are for a particular type of work environment. This factor, not unlike values, becomes more important *after* you get a job, and again may play a role in determining how happy or successful you will be within that work environment. Motivation has to do with how badly you want a particular career and how hard you are willing to work to reach your goal. Are you willing to spend the necessary time, money, and effort to go to school for eight years to become a doctor? The answers to those questions may affect your career choice.

According to John Holland, noted career theorist, most people and most occupations can be organized into six basic personality types or job characteristics. This approach makes a lot of sense, especially during the career exploration stage. Someone who is very detailed-oriented and reacts to change in a thoughtful manner is not going to do well in a work environment characterized by chaos and unpredictability. Ability and motivation aside, these factors will make the difference between being satisfied in your job or being miserable.

ASSESSMENT TESTS ARE ONLY A GUIDE

It's important to remember that assessment tests are only *a guide*. Granted they can be a very revealing guide, but the results are only a snapshot of who a person is at this particular moment in time. Think of these assessment results as just another piece of data gathered along your career decision-making journey.

Just because an interest inventory *says* you should be an architect doesn't mean you *have* to be one. There are many different types of assessment tools that measure different aspects of a person's personality. That's why it's always a good idea to take more than one inventory.

Print out and keep the results of any assessments you take online. Compare the results, and see if there are any patterns. Then talk with a real person about what you've discovered. Traditionally, pencil and paper inventories are only *one part* of the career counseling process

and are usually followed by a meeting with a career counseling professional—someone who can integrate the results, interpret their mean-
ing, and then suggest some career possibilities. With this said, don't
rely on free online assessments alone for career guidance. If you are a
student in college, meet with a career counselor to discuss your results.
If you are in high school, take the test under the guidance and support
of your school counselor.

CHAPTER 4

Self-Assessment Web Sites

INTRODUCTION

There are a multitude of self-assessment questionnaires and inventories on the Internet that measure everything from intelligence to personal compatibility. Interest inventories can be very helpful in identifying a pool of possible occupations that you can explore. Most of the assessments listed in this chapter are fun, insightful, and are presented in an attractive format. Some are offered free of charge through a college career counseling center or as part of a commercial Web site from an employment recruiter, or a corporate, personnel and management consulting organization. Assessment instruments or surveys offered by a commercial, or "for profit" company or organization can give you some interesting results, but they are generally geared for adults already in the workforce or in the corporate world. That doesn't mean that high school and college students cannot obtain some valuable and insightful information from these sites. Just make sure the site is secure, and that you don't inadvertently sign up to pay for something you didn't intend to pay for.

The web sites listed below were selected because they are free of charge (with the exception of the *Self-Directed Search (SDS)* and are appropriate for high school and college students in the career exploration process. The *SDS* was included because it is such a good, reliable tool and the fee is minimal. Some of the more popular standardized interest inventories such as *FIRO-B*, *Myers-Briggs*, *Campbell Interest and Skill Survey*, the *Strong Interest Inventory*, and the *Jackson Vocational Interest Survey* are now available online but charge a fee to use.

GENERAL SELF-ASSESSMENT WEB SITES

The Career Key
http://www.careerkey.org

The Career Key was developed by Lawrence K. Jones, Ph.D. at North Carolina State University. This 66-question vocational test is based on the six Holland personality types. It measures skills, abilities, values, interests, and personality, and will identify promising careers that are linked to career information from the *Occupational Outlook Handbook*.

The Career Interests Game
http://career.missouri.edu

Developed by the University of Missouri Career Center, this "game" is based on John Holland's theory and resembles the *Party Exercise* by Richard N. Bolles. Each Holland type has links to job descriptions, education and training, employment outlook, and salaries from the *Occupational Outlook Handbook*. Select "Career Interests Game" under "Quick Links."

Careerlink
http://www.mpc.edu/cl/climain.htm

Careerlink was developed by the Monterey Peninsula College Career Services. This 36-question assessment generates a career profile which matches self-identified characteristics and preferences (e.g., interests, aptitudes, temperament, physical capacities, preferred working conditions, and desired length of preparation for employment) with those of 80 career clusters. This fun, colorful site relies on an honest self-assessment.

John Holland's Self-Directed Search
http://www.self-directed-search.com

This is the online version of the *Self-Directed Search*, developed by Dr. John L. Holland. The test takes 15 minutes and costs $9.95. The fee includes a printable, personalized report that provides a list of occupations that most closely match your interests.

The Keirsey Temperament Sorter II
http://Keirsey.com

The Keirsey Temperament Sorter is a fun, interesting, and revealing questionnaire that identifies a Rational, Idealist, Artisan, or Guardian temperament. It will also suggest appropriate careers. This 70-question assessment is related to the Myers-Briggs Type Indicator. To use, select on the "Take the Keirsey Sorter" button. The temperament description is free, but there is a charge for the 10-page Character Report and the new Career Report.

The Princeton Review Career Quiz™
http://www.princetonreview.com/cte/

This quiz is a shortened version of *The Birkman Method*. It is brief, only 24 questions, and provides a general description of interests, skills, preferred style (described in terms of "Birkman Colors"), and a list of possible careers. To use, select on "Take the Career Quiz."

TypeFocus™ Personality Profile
http://www.typefocus.com

The Type Focus Personality Profile is a quick and easy 66-question assessment that provides results in the form of Myers-Briggs Personality Types. The assessment is free, but the detailed report is available for a fee. The results and their applicability to the world of work will be more meaningful if discussed with a trained career or guidance counselor. Best for college and senior high school students.

Workplace Values Assessment
http://www.quintcareers.com/workplace_values.html

A short inventory from *Quintcareers.com*. Helps individuals examine what they value in work (e.g., helping society, working under pressure, stability, status, etc).

CHAPTER 5

Career Exploration Web Sites

INTRODUCTION

The second step involved in choosing a career is knowing what's out there in the work world. Most high school students are not ready to make decisions about a career and a major, because they have only been exposed to a limited number of occupations. Even many college students aren't ready to declare a major, simply because they do not have enough information to make a realistic career decision.

To help you explore career options, this chapter is organized into three sections: General Career Exploration Web Sites, Web Sites for High School Students, College Web Sites, and Web Sites Especially for Women and Minority Students.

GENERAL CAREER EXPLORATION SITES

General career exploration Web sites are a good starting place for gathering general career information and exploring options. Some of these sites offer a variety of career-related information such as self-assessments, information about the career planning process, steps to follow in your decision-making journey, and information about majors.

WEB SITES FOR HIGH SCHOOL STUDENTS

Web sites for high school students are directly targeted to the interests and concerns of high school students. Some of these sites contain assessments, career profiles, or magazine articles.

COLLEGE WEB SITES

The *college Web sites*, while certainly not limited to college-aged students, are primarily career and placement center homepages from colleges and universities across the United States. These sites offer a wealth of in-depth information about specific college majors and the careers they can lead to, related career titles, and job projections. High school juniors and seniors will also find these sites invaluable to not only to research individual majors, but to research potential colleges that offer the majors they are interested in. As new jobs and new job titles emerge in the workforce, colleges generally respond by adding and modifying the majors they offer. So by surfing some of these college Web sites, you may discover a new or related major you never knew existed.

AFTER THE SURFING IS OVER

After reviewing several Web sites and completing the self-assessments or other activities they offer, you should be able to identify a couple of general career areas that you're interested in. If you're relatively unde-cided in your choice of major or career, try to select one or two career "clusters" like "Health Care" or "Science." Otherwise, try to narrow your choice to one or two college "majors" or careers (e.g., business or engineering). Don't worry about choosing a speciality area within a major at this time. That will come once you enroll in college and are exposed to courses in your major.

WHAT TO DO IF YOU CAN'T DECIDE ON A MAJOR

If you simply cannot decide on a major, at least try to make the distinc-tion between science-oriented majors or non-science ones. Science-based majors generally require more math and science courses than non-science based majors, which usually require more liberal arts and language courses. The key is to keep as many options open as possible until you are ready to select a particular major. This is very important. Since career development occurs at different rates of speed for differ-ent people, not everyone is ready to make an appropriate career choice when they enter college. Consequently, many students end up going to college longer than four years simply because they changed majors or career directions at some point in time during college.

Changing majors usually results in making up missed courses at the freshman or sophomore level and/or taking additional courses at the junior or senior level in order to complete the graduation requirements of the new major. Many people get upset about having to go to school for more than four years, but there is nothing wrong with this—in fact, it's far better to change your mind, extend your college career, and graduate in something you like, rather than graduating in four years in something you do not enjoy. Generally speaking, it is easier to switch from a science major to a non-science major (with no loss of time) than it is to go from a liberal arts curriculum to a science or engineering major. Some colleges also have "entrance-to-major" requirements for their highly competitive majors. This means that certain courses would have to be completed with a particular grade-point average, prior to applying for entrance into that major.

If you start with a more academically rigorous track, and then decide to major in something like chemistry or physics in your junior or senior year, you may only be looking at one or two additional years to complete your degree. If you began in a liberal arts sequence and *then* decided to switch to chemistry, you may be looking at three or fours more years, or possibly transferring to another school if there are any entrance-to-major restrictions, because of the lack of prerequisite freshman and sophomore level math and science courses (Calculus, Biology, Chemistry, Physics). That's why making this very basic career decision, (a math-based versus a non math-based major) can save you time, money, and aggravation in the long run.

Happy exploring!

GENERAL CAREER EXPLORATION WEB SITES

About
http://www.about.com

About is a network of information about a variety of topics. Visit "Jobs & Careers" for links to articles, feature stories, and career resources.

ISEEK
http://www.iseek.org

This is Minnesota's one-stop site for education, employment, and career resources. Visit "Explore careers" for help with the career planning process, a search tool to find assessments that fit your needs, and information about researching careers and descriptions of specific careers.

Job Hunter's Bible
http://www.jobhuntersbible.com

The web site from Richard Bolles, the author of *What Color Is Your Parachute?* Excellent.

Jobweb
http://www.jobweb.com

Select "Career Library" for an extensive collection of online career exploration resources, articles, and job profiles. Sponsored by the National Association of Colleges and Employers (NACE).

Learn more Resource Center
http://www.learnmoreindiana.org

The Learn more Resource Center provides information about careers and work for high school and college students. This site contains in-house inventories (note the Merkler Style Preference Inventory is licenced for Indiana residents only), a collection of 480 career profiles (a one-minute video, job description, wages, work conditions, licensing requirements, etc), and a great publications list.

My Future
http://www.myfuture.edu.au

Formerly called the Australian Careers Directory, this site is not to be con-fused with the American Web site, *myfuture.com*. This newly updated site offers current information about career development, work and employ-ment, education, funding, and plenty of professional resources.

North Carolina Careers
http://nccareers.org

This is North Carolina's career information system. The "Occupations" section contains extensive information about specific careers, including a descriptive profile, employee characteristics, Holland codes, values, job requirements, work conditions, employment outlook, and professional organizations. "Education & Training" matches occupations to postsecondary training programs. "Career Planning" breaks down the career planning process into five steps. Also contains an "Explore" or assessment section.

O*NET
http://online.onetcenter.org

The Occupational Information Network is an online database that has replaced the *Dictionary of Occupational Titles*. *O*NET* contains detailed descriptions of over 950 occupations, labor market information, career exploration and assessment tools, and the *O*NET* Database. Published by the United States Department of Labor.

Quintessential Careers
http://www.quintcareers.com

A complete resource of career tips, information, and links to the best career and job-related sources. Information and articles on career assessment and college planning. Special sections for high school students, college students, and job seekers. Includes the feature, "Ask the Career Doctor."

Schools in the USA
http://www.schoolsintheusa.com

Not only does this site allow you to search for colleges, but contains a comprehensive collection of nearly 1,000 career profiles. Select "Career Search" for detailed descriptions of careers, typical tasks, salaries, and educational requirements.

Work Futures
http://www.workfutures.bc.ca

This interesting site is British Columbia's Occupational Outlooks. *Work Futures* provides information on career planning, plus a comprehensive description of almost 200 occupations as they relate directly to the British Columbia labor market.

WEB SITES SPECIFICALLY FOR
HIGH SCHOOL STUDENTS

Bureau of Labor Statistics
http://stats.bls.gov/k12/html/edu_over.htm

Occupational descriptions, job titles, and information on math, science, reading, music & arts, social studies, building & fixing things, helping people, law, managing money, sports, and nature. For students K–12. To access this page from the BLS homepage, click on "Kid's Page: Career Information for Kids."

Career Zone
http://www.nycareerzone.org

An excellent career exploration site with exceptional graphics. Use the "flash site" option for optimal results. This is a free, career exploration and planning system especially designed for middle and high school students. In addition to occupational information, it provides access to 300 career videos. Students can even create their own portfolios. Designed by the New York State Department of Labor with a grant from the United States Department of Labor.

College Board
http://www.Collegeboard.com

The College Board online. For a complete resource of information on making the most of high school, preparing for college, and exploring college majors select "For Students," then "Find a College," and finally "Majors & Careers."

I Could Be
http://www.icouldbe.org

A Web site community of mentors and proteges. Connects teens with career mentors over the Internet to help them discover what they could be regarding their career possibilities. *I Could Be* is a national non-profit resource that serves America's underserved teens.

Mapping Your Future
http://www.mapping-your-future.org/planning

A career planning site appropriate for middle, high school, and college students.

Minnesota Careers
http://www.mncareers.org

A nice resource of information and self-assessment forms. Includes information on exploring and investigating careers, job descriptions, and recommended courses in high school. Developed by the Minnesota Department of Employment and Economic Development.

My Future
http://myfuture.com

This is a great resource for high school and college students. Contains information and resources about careers, career assessment, job hunting, finances, and the benefits of a career in the military. Created by the United States Department of Defense.

Next Step Magazine
http://www.nextstepmagazine.com

A magazine written for high school students. Career and college information, interesting articles, and cool links.

Your Vocation
http://www.yourvocation.com

A not-for-profit project whose purpose is to assist today's youth in making informed decisions about their future vocations. Read how others rate their current careers and even email questions.

COLLEGE WEB SITES

America's Career InfoNet
http://www.acinet.org

Although primarily for job seekers, this is an excellent site for researching careers. It features employment trends, occupational requirements, state-by-state labor market conditions, and even career videos for more than 300 occupations.

Career Development Manual
http://www.careerservices.uwaterloo.ca

An exceptional site developed by the University of Waterloo, Ontario, Canada. Contains a Career Development EManual offering plenty of information on the entire career decision-making process as well as self-assessment forms and career exploration exercises.

Career Map
http://www.career.missouri.edu

Career Map lists job titles and employment areas by college major. From the University of Missouri Career Center.

Career Offices Home Pages
http://www.jobweb.com/Career_Development/collegeres.htm

This site contains links to career office homepages at various colleges and universities across the United States. Simply select a college by geographic region. Also has links for colleges in Canada, Australia, and the United Kingdom. Sponsored by *Jobweb.com*.

Career Resource Centre
http://www.umanitoba.ca/student/counselling/crc.html

From the Career Resource Centre at the University of Manitoba. Information on hundreds of occupations and a "What Can I Do with an Undergraduate Degree in..." table.

Choosing a Major: Factors to Consider
http://www.college.upenn.edu/curriculum/major_factors.html

Developed by the University of Pennsylvania. A checklist of things to consider when choosing a major.

Explore Career Planning Options by Major
http://www.rivier.edu/departments/cardev/major/body.htm

An excellent resource for a variety of college majors offered at Rivier College. This site lists skills, job titles, sample employers, ways to increase employability, professional organizations, and major specific career-related Web sites. It also contains a tutorial on how to choose a college major.

Jobweb
http://www.jobweb.com/resources/Library/default.htm

This is Jobweb.com's online article library. There are a variety of career and job-related articles to choose from. Click on "Career Development" for information on what to do to choose a career, and "Majors & Careers" for articles featuring specific jobs and majors.

Major Decisions
http://www.psu.edu/dus/md

From the Division of Undergraduate Studies office at Penn State University. Although this site contains information specifically for Penn State students, it also has information applicable to all students, including common misperceptions about choosing a major.

Major Resource Kits
http://www.udel.edu/CSC/mrk.html

Developed by the Career Service Center at the University of Delaware. A large collection of "kits" on a wide variety of majors. Each kit includes a short description of the major, sample job titles, links to professional resources, and a list of additional resource materials.

Match Major Sheets
http://www.career.fsu.edu/ccis/matchmajor/matchmenu.html

Match occupations with a list of college majors. Provides sample work settings and a list of professional organizations and resources. From the Career Center at Florida State University.

What Can I Do With A Major In...
http://www.ashland.edu/cardev

This is Ashland University's Career Development Center Web site. "Major In Sheets" contains facts about career options, transferrable skills, experiential education, and employment sites. Limited only to the majors offered by the college and it's particular geographic area.

What Can I Do With A Major In...?
http://www.uncwil.edu/stuaff/career/Majors

Created by the University of North Carolina at Wilmington. Select on a particular major for a description and find related career titles, skills needed to be successful in a particular major, and links to major/career specific Web sites. Limited to the majors offered by the school.

What Can I Do With This Major?
http://career.utk.edu

The Career Services at the University of Tennessee at Knoxville offers this convenient Web site, for a nominal fee, using Adobe Acrobat. Select "Students," then "What Can I Do With This Major?" to view career areas, typical employers, strategies to succeed, and resource links for selected majors. Career Services asks that you do not set a link to this site.

WEB SITES ESPECIALLY FOR WOMEN

Cool Jobs for Girls
http://www.work4women.org

An excellent site highlighting nontraditional careers for women and girls. Select on "Cool Jobs for Girls" for information about high wage careers and profiles of women working in cool jobs.

Hard Hatted Women
http://www.hardhattedwomen.org

Begun in 1979, this organization was founded by three women as a support group for women in trade occupations.

WebGrrls International
http://www.webgrrls.com

This web site is "a forum for women interested in new media and technology to network and exchange job and business leads, form strategic alliances, mentor, and learn the skills to help women succeed in an increasingly technical workplace and world." Although primarily for women already in the workforce, the "Career" section does include information and articles on specific careers.

Womens Work
http://www.womenswork.org

A resource center for collaborative work among women. "The Role Model Project for Girls" is a collection of segments in which professional women discuss their careers.

WEB SITES ESPECIALLY FOR MINORITY STUDENTS

The Black Collegian
http://www.black-collegian.com

This site provides cutting-edge information on career resources for students of color. Select "Career Related" for information and articles on a variety of career planning and job-related topics.

Saludos Hispanos
http://www.saludos.com

This site is devoted to promoting the careers and education of the Hispanic community. Select "Career Pavilion" under "Job Seekers" for tips on everything from finding the right career to job search strategies.

CHAPTER 6

Putting It All Together

INTRODUCTION

For those of you who think career counseling ends in high school, welcome to College 101 and the proverbial question, "What's your major?"

The old adage, "Remember you can always change your major," is true more often than not. Research conducted by Penn State University and other institutions has shown that up to 80% of entering college students are not sure of their major, and over 50% of entering freshmen will change their majors at least once before graduation (Division of Undergraduate Studies, 1995).

Most students know very little about the hundreds of career opportunities available to them, or what these careers require or involve. Many of you may hear about a career for the first time by attending a class, from a friend, or at a party. *The Dictionary of Occupational Titles* (DOT) lists over 12,000 occupations. Colleges and universities offer anywhere from 50 to 200 different majors depending on the size of the institution. In addition to knowing the majors colleges offer, you need to learn about the potential kinds of jobs related to those majors. What are the requirements of all of these different programs of study? And how do they related to your own aptitudes and interests? Just reading the college catalogue isn't enough, although it is a good place to start. Before you can make a realistic decision about your major, it's important to take an informed look at all the possibilities.

As you gain more life experience and are exposed to new people, ideas, beliefs, and values, you may find yourself challenging or even rejecting the values of your family and community. You may feel a greater sense of social as well as personal responsibility as you develop higher levels of tolerance and acceptance for people in the world.

With regard to your career choice, your perspective may now include integrating work, family, and leisure. What you once thought was interesting a few years ago may not hold the same appeal anymore. Likewise, what once was so important may now seem trivial as other priorities take its place.

Take advantage of this time and view it as an opportunity to learn about all of the options open to you. Set some long-range and some short-range goals for yourself. A healthy approach is recognizing that indecision is normal and realizing that patience will help you make a good decision.

STRATEGIES FOR DECIDING ON A MAJOR OR CAREER:

- Be actively involved in the decision-making process.
- Get current information. Base your decision on up-to-date employment statistics, information, descriptions, and advice.
- Make a commitment that *you* will make a career decision (even though you may wish someone would do it for you).
- Seriously weigh your values, prioritize what is important to you and your future.
- Be realistic about your abilities. What are your areas of strength? What areas will need more training or development?
- Ask your friends or family members to give you some honest feedback about the type of person you are to gain insight into yourself.
- Use all available resources at school. Make an appointment with your school counselor, a career counselor at a local college, or talk with your teachers. Utilize career resources such as interest inventories, books, magazines, or computerized guidance programs. Use the Internet to research occupations and careers, employment statistics, and explore related career links. Visit not only your school's Web site, but Web sites from other schools, colleges and universities, and professional organizations as well.
- Gain hands-on experience in a field by doing volunteer work, working part or full-time, applying for an internship or co-op (cooperative learning), or study abroad experience. Ask your guidance counselor, teacher, club advisor, or a family member to help you arrange a job shadowing situation where you actually spend time with a professional at his/her work site, or make an appointment to talk with a

human resources manager or a professional employed in the field you wish to consider.

- Take a college course to see if you might like a particular major. Many times you will be able to count this course as an elective if you decide not to pursue it.
- Read books, professional journals, or magazines. Most libraries are excellent sources of professional books and journals.
- Join a student club or organization or just attend an open meeting. Most academic departments establish their own clubs or student chapters of professional organizations. Meeting dates are usually announced via fliers on bulletin boards or in the student newspaper.

6-1 HOW TO CHOOSE A MAJOR

A. Interests (What do I enjoy?)
1. _____
2. _____
3. _____

B. Favorite subjects in school?
1. _____
2. _____
3. _____

C. Abilities and skills (What am I good at?)
1. _____
2. _____
3. _____
4. _____
5. _____

D. Personality style (Describe yourself using adjectives)
_____
_____

E. Work values (What's important to you?) Circle all that apply.
Helping others?	Solving problems?
Using tools/machinery?	Public contact?
Time alone?	Directing others?

Seeing results?	Creativity?
Competition?	Being part of a team?
Independence?	Being accurate?
Physical challenge?	Being rewarded?

F. Family values and expectations?

_____

_____

G. Select 1-3 majors/career areas that include the features you listed in A-E:

1. _____
2. _____
3. _____

Being able to select a specific career from this list will require researching each possible occupation to determine which career is best for you.

6-2   A JOURNEY BACK TO THE PAST (QUESTIONS FOR UNDECIDED STUDENTS)

Try to answer these questions as thoroughly and thoughtfully as you can. See if there are any trends or common themes that can be used to point you toward a possible career. When researching careers or occupations, keep these answers in mind and make some mental comparisons to the jobs or careers you are investigating.

Self-Exploration

1. When you were a child, what did you want to be when you grew up? Why?
2. What did you do for fun? What were your hobbies? Do you still do any of these things today? Why or why not?
3. Did you prefer to play by yourself, with one or two others, or with a large group of people?
4. If you played sports, did you prefer an individual (track, tennis) or team (football, basketball) sport?
5. What things were important to you then? What made you happy?

6. What was your greatest achievement or accomplishment? How did you go about reaching it? How did you feel afterward? What does this tell you about yourself?

7. What subjects did you enjoy in school? In which subjects did you receive your highest grades?

8. Were your strengths in the math/science areas or non-math/science areas. Which area did you enjoy most?

9. Did you have any special talents (art, music, sports)? Are you still pursuing these activities?

10. What did your parents/guardians do for a living? Your grandparents? Aunts/uncles? Other close relatives? How did this influence you?

11. What extracurricular activities did you participate in high school? Which did you enjoy most? Why?

12. What did you typically do after school? On the weekends?

13. What are your strongest personal qualities? What do your friends like the most about you?

14. What are your limitations? What would you like to improve about yourself?

15. Name the highest point in your life. Why was it so special or important?

Academic/Occupational Exploration

1. Which major(s) or career(s) are you considering? List what you like about each. List what you do not like about each.

2. Is this the same major or career you wanted to be when you were young? If not, how is it similar or different? What happened to change your mind?

3. How do feel your abilities fit the requirements needed to succeed in these majors/careers?

4. Will these majors/careers provide the rewards and satisfaction you want for your life? Allow you to achieve what you want out of life? Why?

5. Who or what has influenced your ideas or how you feel about these majors/ careers?

6. List all of the full-time or part-time jobs you had or currently have, and what you liked and did not like about them.

7. If you could create the perfect job, what would it look like? Be as specific as possible, describe it in detail, right down to the type of office decor you would choose.

8. What do you picture yourself doing five years after you graduate from college? Ten years?

9. If you have free time, or a spare hour between classes, what do you typically do? What do you do when you're bored? On the weekends? Over holiday breaks?

10. Are you considering college? Why or why not? What does earning a college degree mean to you?

6-3   HOW TO DEVELOP A CAREER PORTFOLIO

INTRODUCTION

A career portfolio is a collection of career development materials and activities and reflective information. The goal is to demonstrate your personal career development journey from the freshman through senior years by engaging in exploration, investigation, and decision-making activities using the resources available in this book and on the Internet.

The development of the career portfolio begins when you enter school and continues until you graduate.

PURPOSE

The portfolio should be developed in an ongoing manner and is periodically used as a tool for reflection, exploration, and refinement of career decisions. The overall purpose is to actively engage in the career exploration, investigation, decision-making process.

At the end of your senior year it is expected that you will have identified a career goal and developed a plan to reach that goal.

The process of developing a career portfolio also provides opportunities for feedback from family members, faculty advisors, or counselors during each step of the process. Identifying your interests, strengths, values, investigating potential occupations, and setting goals are all important steps in making a sound, informed career decision. Actively engaging in each step of the process will allow you to take charge of your career direction.

The portfolio can also assist you in applying for internships, scholarships, graduate school, or in the job search process.

STRUCTURE

Physically, a portfolio should be a well-organized, attractive presentation of career development materials and activities. It might be organized in paper format (a three-ring binder with tabs, table of contents, etc.), or in digital format (on a disk or CD-ROM).

CONTENT

The portfolio should include the following components:

A. Self Knowledge — Understanding how personal strengths and weaknesses, interests, values, motivations, and abilities enter into career selection.
B. Occupational Exploration and Research — Investigate and explore career options.
C. Career Decision-Making — Consider how the results of your self-assessment and career exploration activities correlate with your future career plans. Select the career or occupation that best matches your personal characteristics.
D. Career Planning — Research the prerequisite skills and educational requirements of your chosen career. Develop an Individual Career Plan to reach that goal. Include personal and educational goals and objectives, activities, and a time line.

SUGGESTED ACTIVITIES

A. Self Knowledge

- Using the Web sites listed in Chapter 4, complete at least two self-assessments or interest inventories. Write a brief report summarizing your findings. Compare and contrast the results. What did you learn about yourself? Include a copy of the results in your portfolio.
- Identify and list your interests, values, motivations, and personality style. Complete the "How To Choose A Major" career sheet in Chapter 6.
- Select a tentative career area using Chapters 8–15 as a reference.

B. Occupational Research

- Explore at least two general career exploration sites listed in Chapter 5. Identify the Web sites and summarize your findings.
- Select and research at least five occupations related to your interests using the Web sites in Chapters 8–15. These occupations may be within one career area or among several career areas. If you are unsure where to begin, use the "If You Enjoy..." career sheet in Chapter 7 as a starting point. Document the Web resources used. Then complete the career sheet, "Questions To Ask Yourself While Researching An Occupation" in Chapter 7.
- Select and conduct a minimum of two of the following activities: informational interview, job shadow, paid or volunteer work, mentor/tutor, co-op or internship experience. Write a brief but detailed report about your experience. Include the name of the company or organization, name and title of the person interviewed or contacted, what you did during the experience, what you learned about yourself and that career, and how it affected your career decision.
- Using the Web sites listed in Chapters 8–15, contact (via phone, e-mail, or in person), a professional in the field you are considering. Use a contact person from one of the career-specific Web sites, or obtain a name from the Web site of a professional organization (hint: access the organization's membership list, if available). Interview that person for specifics about their job, their career path, what they do on a daily basis, what they like and do not like about their job, and their successes and obstacles.
- (Alternative activity) Research a famous person in the profession or occupation of your choice using the Internet. Draw a chart or time line or write a report to show their career path over time, education, tasks, responsibilities, obstacles along the way, accomplishments, and impact on society.

C. Decision-Making

- Narrow your career choice down to one or two specific majors (or a combination of majors and minors).
- Write a self-reflective paper on "Why I Believe This Career Is a Good Choice For Me." Support your decision with the

information you gathered from completing the career sheets in Chapters 6 and 7.

D. Career Planning

- Using the results of the "How To Choose a Major" career sheet in Chapter 6, develop an educational plan that will enable you to reach your career goal. Include the following:

  1. The type of college degree, work experience, and skills needed to enter your chosen career (name of institution, location, program or major, length of time, cost).
  2. The courses and activities you will need to complete (volunteer experience, job shadowing, interviewing, internships, co-op, membership in clubs and organizations, relevant activities in your community, attendance at career fairs, the GRE or other graduate entrance examinations, certification tests, application for further training or application to other colleges/universities or graduate schools).
  3. A description of your ideal professional job. Refer to the results of your self-assessment and "Questions To Ask Yourself While Researching an Occupation" and "Some Final Questions to Ask Yourself" in Chapter 7.
  4. Your future professional goals.

Document the resources used. Review your plan with at least one adult. Refine your career plan as needed.

Questions Students Should Ask Themselves While They Surf

WHY SOME OF US DO NOT CHOOSE WISELY

Many of us have heard stories about people who picked the wrong major, or found themselves in careers they later did not enjoy. Although there are many reasons for this, lack of appropriate career information and lack of self-awareness are probably the most critical reasons.

Students receive advice from many people, including their families, about what they *should* do with their lives before they have made that decision for themselves. Sometimes young people are overly influenced by what they read or watch on television. Perhaps the most common reason for poor career choice is when there is a disconnect between what a student wants to do and where their strengths lie. When I was in high school, many of us wanted to become veterinarians after reading James Herriot's best seller, *All Creatures Great and Small,* even though we did not have the academic qualifications to be successful. As a college advisor, I saw several students who wanted to change their major to pre-law after watching *JAG.* Think about how many students want to be professional athletes and the infinitesimally small number of athletes that actually make it to the professional level.

Second to not knowing who you are and want you want from your personal and work life is lack of information. Without taking an informed look at all career possibilities, it is difficult to make a realistic decision about your major or career. Many students happily complete a major in college only to go into the work world and find out their job was not all they expected it to be.

Other students sometimes select, or are advised to select, majors or careers based on only a small piece of information. Think about how many people pick engineering simply because they're "good at math." The field of engineering is much more than *just math*. And while engineering may be an appropriate option for someone who has an affinity for math, there are hundreds of other math-related careers and jobs that may be just as rewarding. That's why occupational research is so important.

HOW TO BEGIN RESEARCHING CAREERS

As you begin researching careers, make a list of the ones that you are interested in and that seem to best fit your values, personality style, and skills and abilities. Once you've selected several options, go back and research their educational requirements. What major (or majors) do you need to take in college? What type of degree is required? Will additional schooling or training beyond a bachelor's degree be required? If you're in middle or high school, find out what courses you will need to take in high school to prepare you for the postsecondary training you'll need to complete after high school. In other words, look into the future and identify your career goal. Then work your way back through college or high school to whatever educational level you are now, and map out the direction you need to go and what courses you'll need to take to eventually reach that goal. And remember, in some cases, *several* majors or degrees may lead to the same destination.

COLLEGE MAJORS AND CAREERS

If you are in the process of researching college majors, you will notice that some majors are designed to prepare you for a specific profession. These majors are called *Professional Degrees*. Examples of professional careers are doctors, lawyers, nurses, veterinarians, surveyors, physical therapists, occupational therapists, speech pathologists, and chiropractors. Professional degrees usually require study beyond a four year degree.

Other college majors are designed to prepare you for a variety of jobs within a broad occupational field, such as business, engineering, art, science, agriculture. Then there are majors that don't necessarily prepare you for any *one* thing, but are pathways to a variety of careers. Many of these examples can be found in the humanities or liberal arts fields. Individuals in these majors are educated in a certain way or have particular skills that can serve them well in a variety of occupations. Granted, some of these jobs may not be as clearly defined, or as familiar, as a career like pre-med, but with a little ingenuity, you can find career applications almost anywhere. For example, a major in speech communications can lead you to careers in law, human resources, a corporate communications specialist, public relations, fund raising, college admissions, sales, and basically any job that requires the ability to verbally express oneself a variety of situations. Likewise, philosophy majors can find employment in education, law, journalism, communications, public affairs, and government work.

You can also combine majors to make yourself more marketable or more qualified for different job settings. This is why colleges and universities offer minors and certificates in addition to standard majors. A major in Spanish combined with business, economics, hotel and restaurant management, business administration, or even health care and counseling can make you very marketable in today's global business world.

Most jobs are made up of more than one discipline, or "knowledge area." For example, actuarial science is really a combination of business and math; graphic design requires both art and computers; Journalism is mass media or communications plus writing or photography; chemical engineering applies the principles of chemistry to the field of engineering (math and physics), and a position as college president can be a combination of speech communication, public relations, business management, education, psychology, and philosophy.

There are also many different types of work settings or applications within the same job or career. Students sometimes think if they major in XYZ they will be locked into only one type of job. The reality is that people have more freedom than they realize to choose the environment that meets their needs and fits their personality type. Someone interested in chemistry has the choice of working in a lab or research setting, as a pharmacist (a customer service application), or as an educator in a high school or college. It is in the fine nuances of a work environment that a person's values and personality type play a role in determining whether you're going to enjoy or not enjoy a job. If you like to work with people, you can apply your love of people to a variety of work environments. For example, you can work with people in a health care capacity (doctor, nurse), a rehabilitation capacity (physical or occupational therapy, speech pathology), in the schools (teacher, teacher aide, principal, college professor, director of student activities), in an office or

corporate setting (receptionist, human resources, outplacement specialist), or in a social services setting (social worker, counselor, parole
officer, unemployment specialist). People shift their careers around all
the time, in different stages of their careers. An emergency room nurse
who no longer wants to deal with the stress of a hospital emergency
room may decide to apply her skills and experience in a classroom, edit-
ing a journal, or doing research.

WHERE DO I START?

The point is that there are lots of career options. But you have to start
somewhere. The following list provides suggestions for majors or
careers depending on some general interests and abilities. For example, if you love art, but don't know what you can do with an art
degree, this list may suggest some college majors, careers, or jobs
worth investigating. High school students may find this chart more
useful than college students, because it is organized according to subjects familiar to high school students.

Once you have selected an area of interest, follow up by researching not only that particular career, but any related career as well, via
the Web sites in Chapters 8–15. Then complete your research by
answering the questions in the career sheets at the end of this chapter.

Table 7-1

If You Enjoy....	Consider A Career In.....
Animals	Agriculture
	Animal Breeder, Trainer
	Animal Science, Research
	Marine Biology
	Nature/Environmental Educator
	Veterinary Science, Veterinary Assistant
	Wildlife & Fisheries Science
	Zoology
Art	Architecture
	Advertising
	Art Director (Theater, Cinema)
	Art Education

Table 7-1 *(Continued)*

If You Enjoy....	Consider A Career In.....
	Art History
	Art Critic, Appraiser
	Artist
	Advertising
	Cartoonist
	Fashion Designer
	Graphic Artist
	Interior Decorator
	Landscape Architecture
	Medical, Technical, Book Illustrator
	Printing
	Web Site Designer
Children	Administration of Justice
	Criminal Justice
	Counseling
	Child Care, Day care
	Child Psychology
	Early Childhood Education
	Educational Psychology
	Elementary Education
	Health & Human Development
	Pediatric Nurse or Physician
	Social Work
Computers	Computer Engineering
	Computer Science, Programming
	Database Manager
	Data Entry
	Graphic Design
	Information Science & Technology
	Management Information Systems (Business)
	Medical Transcriptionist
	Secretarial Science
	Software Designer
	Surveying
	Webmaster, Designer

(Continued)

Table 7-1 *(Continued)*

If You Enjoy....	Consider A Career In.....
Environment	Agriculture Biology
	Civil Engineering
	Earth Science
	Environmental Education
	Environmental Engineering
	Forest Science
	Geography
	Geosciences
	Landscape Architecture
	Landscaping
	Meteorology
	Mineral Sciences
	Recreation & Parks Management
	Urban Design & Planning
Food or Nutrition	Culinary Arts Instructor
	Baker, Chef, Food Production
	Dietician
	Food Science
	Hotel/Restaurant Management
	Nutrition Consultant, Educator
	Sales
History	Archeology
	Cultural Studies
	Government
	History Teacher
	Historic Site Administrator
	Librarian (further study needed)
	Museum Curator
	Political Science
Languages	Bilingual Education
	College Professor
	Foreign Correspondent, Analyst
	Government
	International Business, Law, Politics
	Linguistics
	Political Science

Table 7-1 *(Continued)*

If You Enjoy....	Consider A Career In.....
	Public Relations
	Translator
Law	Administration of Justice
	Court Reporter
	Criminal Justice
	Conflict Resolution/Mediator
	Human Resources
	Law, Paralegal, Legal Assistant
	Police Officer
	Political Lobbyist
	Political Science
Math	Accounting
	Actuarial Science
	Astronomy
	Astrophysics
	Banking
	Chemistry
	Computer Science
	Economics
	Engineering
	Engineering Technology
	Finance
	Mathematics
	Math or Science Education
	Meteorology
	Physics
	Statistics
	Surveying
	Tax Auditor, Advisor
Music	Conductor
	Music Teacher
	Music Therapist
	Professional Performer
	Public Relations Director
	Recording Engineer, Technician

(Continued)

Table 7-1 (Continued)

If You Enjoy....	Consider A Career In.....
People	Audiology
	Chiropractic
	Counseling
	Dentistry
	Gerontology
	Education
	Human Development
	Human Resources/Labor Specialist
	Law
	Medicine
	Medical Technology
	Mediator
	Nursing
	Police, Firefighter, EMT
	Physical Therapy
	Psychology
	Occupational Therapy
	Receptionist
	Recreational Therapy
	Secretary
	Social Work
Public Speaking	Broadcast Communications
	(Radio/TV)
	Business
	Corporate Training
	Education (any level)
	Law
	Public Relations
	Sales
	Speech Communications
Science	Agriculture
	Animal Sciences
	Biology
	Biochemistry
	Bioengineering
	Chemistry

Table 7-1 *(Continued)*

If You Enjoy....	Consider A Career In.....
	Education
	Forensics
	Geneticist
	Horticulture
	Microbiology
	Molecular Biology
	Medical Technology
	Medicine
	Nursing
	Pharmacy or Pharmaceutical Sales
	Physician Assistant
	Speech Pathology
	Veterinarian, Veterinary Assistant
	Zoology
Sports	Athletic Trainer
	Coach, Athletic Director
	Golf Course Manager
	Exercise Science, Kinesiology
	Health Club Owner
	Physician
	Personal Trainer
	Physical Therapy
	Sports Analyst/Commentator
	Sports Medicine
	Sporting Goods Sales, Marketing
	Sports Writer
	Teacher/Coach
	Therapeutic Recreation Therapist
Working With Your Hands	Artesian or Craftsperson
	Auto Mechanic
	Carpentry
	Construction
	Culinary or Food Preparation

(Continued)

Table 7-1 (Continued)

If You Enjoy....	Consider A Career In.....
	Data Entry Clerks
	Drafting
	Electrician
	Engineering, Engineering Technology
	Farmer (Animals, Fruits, Vegetables)
	Heating, Plumbing
	Heavy Equipment Operator
	Landscaping/Nursery Owner
	Manufacturing
	Machinist
	Medical Technology
	Printing
	Surveying, Surveying Technology
	Trucking
	Watch, Jewelry Repair
Writing	Advertising, Marketing
	English, Creative Writing Teacher
	Editor, Publisher
	Journalist
	Paralegal
	Public Relations
	Technical Writer, Editor

QUESTIONS TO ASK YOURSELF WHILE YOU SURF

The following worksheet contains questions you should ask yourself while researching occupations on the Internet. The questions are designed to help you focus your research activities and to think about how well they personally match the occupation you are researching. This worksheet can also be used for other career exploration activities such as job shadowing, business or industry tours, informational interviews, and even job interviews.

7-1   QUESTIONS TO ASK YOURSELF WHILE RESEARCHING AN OCCUPATION

Job Title: _____

Responsibilities: _____

_____

_____

_____

(What are the daily tasks and responsibilities expected of an employee in this job? Does the job require you to work with people, data, machines or ideas?)

Work Conditions: _____

_____

_____

_____

(What are the hours? Is this primarily daytime, evening, or weekend work? Will you be working inside or outdoors? Is travel a part of the job? Will you be expected to work overtime? Where is the job located? Is the job in a manufacturing, retail, office, or clinical setting? What equipment is needed to perform the job? Will you be part of a team or expected to work independently? How much autonomy or decision-making ability will you have? Is it a fast-paced or slower-paced working environment? Will you be expected to perform under pressure or meet deadlines? What is the general social and cultural climate of the workplace?)

Education or Training Needed: _____

_____

_____

(What are the minimal entry-level requirements? What degrees, training, certificates, or work experience are needed? Are there any special personal attributes or physical requirements needed?)

Earnings: _____

(What is the starting wage or salary? Are there opportunities for advancement? What do you have to do, learn, or earn to be successful in this job?)

Employment Outlook: _____

_____

(How many openings will there be when you graduate? Will the openings be competitive? What is the outlook in the next five or ten years? How will these jobs be affected by a globablizing marketplace? By social, political, or economic events?)

List some advantages of working in this job: _____

_____

_____

_____

_____

List some disadvantages: _____

_____

_____

_____

How well does this job match who you are?

_____

_____

_____

7-2 SOME FINAL QUESTIONS TO ASK YOURSELF

- Will I find this job interesting?
- Can I see myself doing this job all day? For several years?
- Do I have the ability to earn the degree or complete the training that's required for this career?
- How successful do I think I will be in this career/profession?
- Do I have the motivation to take the necessary time or academic courses/training to enter this job or career?
- How will I like the working environment? Will the working conditions and people suit me? How well does this work environment match my personality style? How happy or unhappy will I be under these work conditions? Will this environment allow me to grow personally and professionally?
- Is this job or work environment consistent with my values and beliefs?

If you answered "yes," to any of these questions, make sure you can cite solid reasons to support your answer. Likewise, if you answered "no" to any of these questions, understand why you answered the way you did. Is there an alternative way to approach or design this career so that it will meet your needs? Do you need to combine several careers? Finally, if what you love to do is not a feasible career possibility, can you adopt it as a hobby, or "avocation" and choose something else that will allow you to economically survive?

Discuss your results with your parents, a friend, teacher, or counselor to make sure you are considering all factors. If you find you answered "no" more times than "yes", then consider discarding this career choice as a possible career or occupation. If this is the case, then you have made a good decision at this point in your life. Select another career or occupation and continue with your investigation.

CHAPTER 8

Career Sites by Occupational Fields

INTRODUCTION

Hopefully you've been able to narrow your career decision down to one or two occupations or majors. Now it's time to further refine your search by getting into the specifics of each career.

Begin exploring possible careers by selecting an occupational area of interest in one of the following chapters. Each chapter is organized by career clusters. A career cluster is a group of occupations that are related to each other.

If you are not sure where to begin, refer to the chart in Chapter 7 for a suggestion of possible careers based on your interests or abilities. If you already have a specific career in mind, like chemistry, then you can go directly to the appropriate chapter (e.g., math and science, Chapter 15) and begin looking at the Web sites listed under Chemistry.

When you have finished reading all the information available about a particular career, complete the career sheet, "Questions Students Should Ask Themselves While They Surf" in Chapter 7. Spend some time thinking about the questions and answer them as honestly and as completely as you can. Remember, short of actually doing the job, your ability to make an solid career decision will only be as good as the information you gather.

GENERAL CAREER SITES

About My Job
http://www.aboutmyjob.com

This site contains a collection of stories told by people about their jobs.

Best Careers for Black Women in 2000
http://www.dogonvillage.com/Tidbits/bestcareers.htm

This is an article by Alicia Barclay in *Noir Magazine* listing the eight best careers for black women based on demand and salary. Jobs are broken down by title, description, salary, and training.

Black Career Women
http://www.bcw.org

This Web site addresses the needs of black women in the workforce. "Career Assessment" offers a free career analysis and "Careers" contains career-related information.

Career Guide to Industries
http://www.bls.gov/oco/cg

A comprehensive guide to career information by industry. From the Department of Labor.

Job Profiles
http://www.jobprofiles.org

Workers share their stories regarding their work experiences. Read about the rewards, stresses, required basic skills, challenges, and advice on entering a particular field.

Jobs of the Workplace
http://cord.org/workplacelibrary/indices/jobs.html

Highlights jobs people have and how they got there. Covers jobs from agriculture to service technician. Also features personal profiles.

Women's Career and Professional Organizations
http://www.feminist.com/resources/links/links_work.html

This page is sponsored by *Feminist.com* and contains an extensive list of resources for women. There are general career links as well as career-specific professional organizations. You can also search for sites according to topics of interest.

CAREER-SPECIFIC SITES

Careers in Science and Engineering
http://www.nap.edu/readingroom/books/careers/contents.html

This is an online version of a student planning guide to careers in science and engineering written by the *National Academies of Science, Engineering, and Medicine*. Contains information and strategies to meet career goals, survival skills and personal attributes needed to succeed, education required for various careers, tips for finding a job, student scenarios, and career profiles.

Guidance Resources Homepage
http://www.wisemantech.com/guidance

An excellent collection of Web-based career resources developed by the former guidance director at Carl Sandburg High School. Select "Specific Career Information" to learn about career opportunities in a variety of fields from animal behavior to paleontology.

The Internet Public Library
http://www.ipl.org/div/aon

A collection of over 2,000 Internet sites of professional and trade associations organized by occupational field.

North Carolina Careers
http://nccareers.org

This is North Carolina's career information system. The "Occupations" section contains extensive information about specific careers including a descriptive profile, employee characteristics, Holland codes, values, job requirements, work conditions, employment outlook, and professional organizations.

O*NET
http://www.doleta.gov/programs/onet

Online version of the *Dictionary of Occupational Titles*. Contains detailed descriptions of jobs and occupations. Features career exploration and assessment tools and the O*NET Database. Published by the U.S. Department of Labor.

Vocational Information Center
http:// www.khake.com/page2.html

An outstanding collection of vocational and technical career links. Contains career descriptions as well as links to educational sites relating to specific careers. Useful for both teachers and students.

PROFESSIONAL ORGANIZATIONS

Many of the web sites in Chapters 9 through 15 are professional organizations affiliated with a particular career or occupation. They may contain career-specific information about their respective profession, career opportunities, professional activities, and a wealth of other information related to that profession. Included also are non-profit sites containing interesting, career-specific information about a particular occupation. This is not an exhaustive list by any means. For a complete listing of professional associations and organizations, log into *The Internet Public Library* at *http://www.ipl.org/div/aon*.

Keep in mind that most national organizations also have state and local chapters. Contacting your state or local chapter may provide you with additional information or connect you with a professional in your area. Joining a student chapter can be a great way to learn about a profession. It can also provide you with a way to network with professionals in the field which may later lead to internship, co-op, or employment opportunities.

CHAPTER 9

Agriculture and Natural Resources Web Sites

THE AGRICULTURE AND NATURAL RESOURCES CAREER CLUSTER

The Agriculture and Natural Resources career cluster includes occupations concerned with research and application of scientific knowledge to specific problems and situations. People in these occupations generally have interests and skills in *ideas*. They usually have good research and problem-solving skills, and do well in one or more scientific subjects, such as biology or science.

Some of these occupations, such as farming, fishing, and forestry deal with the production, propagation, and gathering of animals, animal products, and plants. People in these occupations usually have interests and skills in *things* and *data*. They generally value nature, working outdoors, and common sense. They often work independently and are straightforward and self-reliant.

AGRICULTURE

Florida Agriculture
http://www.florida-agriculture.com

Explore the world of agricultural science by visiting "Careers in Ag Science" located in the "Consumers" section. Brought to you by the Florida Department of Agriculture and Consumer Services.

Future Farmers of America
http://www.ffa.org

The mission of the Future Farmers of America organization is to prepare students for careers in agriculture. For career information, select "Student Members," then "Explore Careers in Ag." A new searchable database will allow you to explore career fields and areas of employment.

National Agricultural Day
http://www.agday.org

Select "Ag Day Education," then "Careers in Agriculture" for information about the 12 major areas of employment within the field of agriculture. This site was selected as a *USA TODAY* Education Best Bet Web Site, February 26–March 4, 2002.

AGRICULTURAL ENGINEERING (SEE ENGINEERING)

AGRONOMY

American Society of Agronomy
http://www.agronomy.org

This is the official Web site for the American Society of Agronomy (ASA) which was founded in 1907. The "Career Placement" section contains career information and free brochures. The home page for the Students of Agronomy, Soils and Environmental Sciences (SASES) is located in the "Undergraduates"section.

Council for Agricultural Science and Technology
http://www.cast-science.org

This site hosts articles and publications and current information about food, agricultural, and environmental issues. To access career information, select "Programs and Education, then "Science Education."

Crop Science Society of America (CSSA)
http://www.crops.org

CSSA is an educational and scientific organization dedicated to the advancement of crop science. This organization provides a newsletter, a calendar, and meeting details. Visit "Career/Placement" for career information.

ANIMAL SCIENCE

American Society of Animal Science
http://www.asas.org

The ASAS is the professional organization for animal scientists. Visit "Student Info" for career information and links to colleges and universities offering undergraduate and graduate programs in animal science. "Links" contains Web sites of related animal science organizations such as the American Dairy Science and Poultry Science Associations.

NATURAL RESOURCES

ENTOMOLOGY

Entomological Society of America
http://www.entsoc.org

This Web site contains articles and an online journal. Visit "Resources" for college and career-related information.

ENVIRONMENT

EE-Link
http://eelink.net

Sponsored by the North American Association for Environmental Education, this site is a collection of Web resources and links. Visit "EE Student Resources" for links to EE-related information, activities, and games for students interested in the environment.

Environmental Career Resources
http://www.umanitoba.ca/student/counselling/planner/careers/spotlights/environ.html

From the Career Resource Center at the University of Manitoba, Canada. This Web site has a listing of environmental career resources on the Web.

Environmental Careers Organization
http://www.eco.org

"Career Center" contains tips, links, and environmental career resources. "Career Feature" highlights different environmental careers.

Princeton University Outdoor Action
http://www.princeton.edu/~oa/jobs/careeroe.html

A guide to outdoor/environmental careers written by the Director of the Outdoor Action Program at Princeton University.

FISH & GAME

Federal Wildlife Officers Association
http://www.fwoa.org

The Federal Wildlife Officers Association, Inc. is open to all federal law enforcement officers and those who support protecting wildlife.

National Wildlife Federation
http://www.nwf.org

The National Wildlife Federation is the nation's largest member-supported conservation group. Supports school and community programs, environmental education, and advocacy. Check out the "For kids and Teens" for colorful, fun activities for kids.

US Fish and Wildlife Service
http://www.fws.gov

Visit the "Kids/Educators" section for publications, resources, maps, pictures, and videos for students and educators.

FOOD SCIENCE

Institute of Food Technologists
http://www.ift.org

"Introduction to the Food Industry" provides an excellent overview of the field. To view, select "Continuing Education & Professional

Development," then "Career Guidance Resources." The Institute of Food Technologists offers scholarships, fellowships, descriptions of universities offering graduate programs in food science, as well as information about its student organization.

FORESTRY

Forestry Colleges
http://www.forestrycolleges.com/index.html

This site contains general information and facts about forestry, choosing a forestry school, and links to resources.

Society of American Foresters
http://www.safnet.org/index.shtml

This Web site contains a lot of good information about forestry. The "Education" button includes a "Forestry as a Major" article which discusses pursuing a career in forest resources. The "About Forestry" button contains forestry information and links appropriate for both kids and adults.

GENETICS

American Society of Human Genetics
http://www.ashg.org

Visit "Educational Resources" for information on human genetic definitions, careers, and training opportunities.

Careers in the Genetics Field
http://www.faseb.org/genetics/gsa/careers/bro-menu.htm

Articles and profiles about people working in the genetics field.

Genetics Society of America
http://www.genetics-gsa.org

Information on meetings, careers, and publications from this society for scientists and academics.

GEOGRAPHY

Association of American Geographers
http://www.aag.org

This is the Web site of the Association of American Geographers (AAG), a scientific and educational society founded in 1904. Select "Jobs/Careers" for information on careers in geography.

GEOLOGY

American Geophysical Union
http://www.agu.org

The American Geophysical Union is a research organization to promote the "...understanding of Earth and space for the benefit of humanity." The "Science & Society" section provides articles of interest on various issues in geophysics, including a description of the four fundamental areas of the geophysical sciences. Within this same section visit "Careers in Science" for information on careers in earth and space science.

American Institute of Professional Geologists
http://www.aipg.org/ScriptContent/index.cfm

Founded in 1963, this organization certifies practicing geologists and advocates on behalf of the profession. "About AIPG" contains topics covering everything from why you should become a member to policies and ethics. Within this section, visit "Speciality Fields of Practice" for an exhaustive list of specializations within this profession.

American Society of Limnology and Oceanography
http://www.aslo.org

This site offers a "Students" section (located at the bottom of the page) which describes careers in aquatic sciences as well as other student opportunities.

Association for Women Geoscientists
http://www.awg.org

This organization was developed to encourage the participation of women in the geosciences, exchange educational, technical, and professional information, and enhance the professional growth and advancement of women in the geosciences.

Geological Society of America
http://www.geosociety.org

The Geological Society of America was established in 1888. Some of the highlights of this Web site included a bookstore, newsroom, professional resources, and a student section.

Society for Exploration Geophysicists
http://www.seg.org

This society fosters the practice of geophysics in the exploration of natural resources. Visit "You & Geophysics" for information about geophysics, and "...for Students" for more career information, scholarships, student membership, and a kid's section.

HORTICULTURE

American Society for Horticultural Science
http://www.ashs.org

This site features "Who's Who," meetings and events, news, publications, and related Web sites. The "Careers" section profiles career opportunities and lists colleges and universities offering degrees in horticulture science.

LANDSCAPE

American Association of Botanical Gardens and Arboreta
http://www.aabga.org

The AABGA Web site offers publications, resources, meeting information, and a list of public gardens.

American Nursery & Landscape Association
http://www.anla.org

Learn all about the nursery and landscape business by selecting "About the Industry."

Turfgrass Producers International
http://www.lawninstitute.com

See "Links" for an extensive list of career-related associations.

LANDSCAPE ARCHITECTURE (SEE ARTS AND COMMUNICATION)

VETERINARY SCIENCE

American Animal Hospital Association
http://www.healthypet.com

This entertaining Web site is brought to you from the American Animal Hospital Association. Features a pet care library, FAQ's, pet care resources, a hospital search, and a coloring page for kids.

American Veterinary Medical Association
http://www.avma.org

The AVMA is the professional organization for veterinarians. Journals, articles, educational resources, veterinary market statistics, and more.

North American Veterinary Technician Association
http://www.navta.net

An organization for veterinary technologists. To learn what a vet tech is and does, visit "Vet Tech as a Career."

CHAPTER 10

Arts and Communications Web Sites

THE ARTS AND COMMUNICATIONS CAREER CLUSTER

This cluster includes occupations concerned with the creating and performing of artistic works in various forms. Generally, people in artistic occupations have interests and skills in *ideas* and *people*, those in communications occupations have interests and skills in *data* and/or *things*. Many value creativity and independence. They are skilled in creative thinking and are very expressive in nature. Many have aptitudes in art, music, writing, performance, public speaking, and presenting information.

ARTS & THEATER

Art Careers
http://www.uncwil.edu/stuaff/career/Majors/art.htm

An excellent summary of art-related career titles, related skills, and Web resources. From the University of North Carolina, Wilmington.

Careers in the Arts
http://www.oswego.edu/student/career/careersin/index.html

For descriptions of more than 50 art-related careers select "Arts" from the list of careers on this page. From Career Services at the State University of New York at Oswego.

ARCHITECTURE

The American Institute of Architects
http://www.aia.org

This is the Web site of the professional organization for architects. To gain insights into the profession visit "Architects & the Public" and "Practice of Architecture."

Society of Architectural Historians
http://www.sah.org

The Society of Architectural Historians (SAH) promotes the preservation of significant architectural monuments. A list of graduate programs in architectural history can be found under "Student Resources."

ARCHITECTURAL ENGINEERING (SEE ENGINEERING)

DANCE

National Dance Teachers Association
http://www.ndta.org.uk

Visit "Careers in Dance" for information on the wide variety of jobs that are connected to dance in some way. A United Kingdom Web site.

DRAFTING (SEE ENGINEERING)

GRAPHIC ARTS

American Institute of Graphic Arts
http://www.aiga.org

For career information and advice on submitting portfolios,visit the student section located under "Ideas for" drop-down box.

MUSIC

The American Society of Composers, Authors, and Publishers
http://www.ascap.com

This is a professional association of composers, songwriters, lyricists, and music publishers of every kind of music. Visit "Career Development" for articles and advice about the intricacies of the music business.

Women at the Piano
http://www.pianowomen.com

Profiles of over 300 classical women pianists from 1750 to the present.

Women in Music
http://www.womeninmusic.com

For descriptions of careers in the music industry and related resources, select "Home," then scroll down to "Careers & Jobs in Music."

PRODUCERS, DIRECTORS, ACTORS

International Society for the Performing Arts Foundation
http://www.ispa.org

A not-for-profit international organization founded in 1949 for executives and directors of the performing arts.

Producers Guild of America
http://www.producersguild.org

The premier resource for producers of motion pictures and television.

LANDSCAPE ARCHITECTURE

American Society of Landscape Architects
http://www.asla.org

The Web site of the American Society of Landscape Architects. "Career Resources" contains information about careers in landscape architecture, the *Landscape Architecture Interest Test*, and a list of colleges and universities that offer landscape architecture programs.

Association of Professional Landscape Designers
http://www.apld.org

The mission of this organization is to advance landscape designers as an independent profession and recognize them as professionals. Visit "Education" for a list of educational institutions offering programs and courses in the landscape design field. This site also features an extensive list of links for the serious gardener or garden designer.

PHOTOGRAPHY

American Society of Media Photographers
http://www.asmp.org

The American Society of Media Photographers (ASMP) was founded in 1944. Originally called the Society of Magazine Photographers and later the American Society of Magazine Photographers, ASMP is a trade organization which promotes photographers' rights, educates photographers, and produces business publications. This site offers a searchable database for locating a photographer, news, and information related to the media photography profession.

National Press Photographers Association
http://www.nppa.org/default.cfm

Articles, products, and services for professional photographers.

Professional Photographers of America
http://www.ppa.com

An organization for photojournalists. Includes current events, feature articles, contests, and services for members.

Student Photographic Society
http://www.studentphoto.com

Features artists, a newsletter, and a variety of helpful tips on everything from copyright issues to pricing your photos. Must be a member to access some of the areas.

THEATRE

American Association of Community Theatre
http://www.aact.org

Visit this Web site for news and information and about community theatre. Choose "Resources" for arts organizations, job listings, play sources, and theatre terms.

Screen Actors Guild
http://www.sag.org

Read about the latest issues and news concerning the screen acting industry. Visit the "FAQs" page for information about becoming a professional actor.

COMMUNICATIONS

The Association for Women in Communications
http://www.womcom.org

This association provides networking and professional development opportunities to its members. Supports first amendment rights, a free press, and gender equity.

BROADCASTING

The National Association of Broadcasters
http://www.nab.org

NAB represents the interests of free, over-the-air radio and television broadcasters. The "Career Center" offers a variety of career and employment-related information.

The Society of Broadcast Engineers
http://www.sbe.org

Technical information, newsletter, and certification information.

Society of Operating Cameramen
http://www.soc.org

This organization strives to advance the art and creative contribution of camera operators in the motion picture and television industry.

JOURNALISM

American Society of Journalists and Authors
http://www.asja.org

Learn about issues and events in the freelance writing industry at this Web site. "For Writers" has a list of Web resources and professional organizations for writers of various genres.

The American Society of Newspaper Editors
http://www.asne.org

The "Careers" section offers career and employment advice and several very informative articles about preparing for a career in newspapers. The sister site is *http://www.highschooljournalism.org*.

Society of Professional Journalists
http://www.spj.org

Visit "Careers" for career advice, scholarships, fellowships, and employment opportunities in the field of journalism.

PUBLIC RELATIONS

Public Relations Society of America
http//www.prsa.org

Read about careers in public relations by visiting the "Resources"section.

REPORTERS AND CORRESPONDENTS

Radio and Television News Directors Association
http://www.rtndf.org

This organization represents local and network news executives in the broadcasting, cable, and other electronic media. Current events and internship opportunities are also featured. Available in Spanish.

SPEECH COMMUNICATION

American Communication Association
http://www.americancomm.org

This Web site features communication-related news, events, and an online journal. For a collection of online resources, select "Communication Studies Center."

International Speech Communication Association
http://www.isca-speech.org

The goal of this organization is to promote international speech communication, science, and technology.

National Communication Association
http://www.natcom.org

This is the oldest and largest national organization for the communication discipline. Learn about undergraduate and graduate programs and student chapters.

WRITING AND TECHNICAL WRITING

The Modern Language Association
http://www.mla.org

The professional organization and author of the MLA-style documentation guidelines.

Society of Technical Communications
http://www.stc.org

Learn what technical communication is through this web site. Formerly the *Society of Technical Writers and Publishers.*

Writer's Resource Center
http://www.poewar.com

Created in 1993, The Writer's Resource Center is a comprehensive source of internet resources for freelance writers. This site features articles covering everything from general writing issues to poetry to the business side of writing. For information on writing careers, visit "Articles" then select "Glossary of Writing Careers" in the "The Writing Business" column.

CHAPTER 11

Business, Management, and Information Technology Web Sites

THE BUSINESS, MANAGEMENT, AND INFORMATION TECHNOLOGY CAREER CLUSTER

The Business, Management and Information Technology career cluster includes occupations primarily concerned with planning, organizing and controlling specialized operational functions. People in these occupations generally have interests and skills in *data* and *people*. They usually have good analytical, problem-solving and/or good interpersonal skills. Their work may include examining, analyzing, reviewing, purchasing, enforcing and/or personnel responsibilities

Management occupations include top level managers and middle managers. Top level managers are concerned with policy making, planning, staffing, directing and/or controlling activities that are common to many organizations. Middle managers plan, organize, staff, or direct activities at an operational level. People in these occupations usually have interests and skills in *people* and *data*. Many have leadership qualities and possess a high degree of creative thinking, decision-making and problem-solving abilities.

Office and administrative support occupations are concerned with preparing, transcribing, and preserving written and electronic communications and records including the collection, gathering, and dissemination of information. People in these occupations usually have interests and skills in *data* and have to operate various types of office equipment. They often have to participate as a member of a team, and perform their duties with close attention to detail and a high level of accuracy. Those interacting with the public need good communication skills.

Sales and marketing occupations are concerned with selling goods and services and purchasing commodities and property for resale. People in these occupations usually have interests and skills in *people* and often are persuasive in nature. They value success, status, initiative, and are often described as ambitious, outgoing, and enthusiastic. They are skilled in speaking, listening, and must effectively serve their clients and customers.

Library science is also included in this cluster because it deals with information technology. Librarians make information available to people in libraries. They also help people find the information they need via computerized databases. Other duties which they may perform include: supervising staff, preparing budgets, repairing materials, and handling special collections.

BUSINESS & ADMINISTRATION

American Business Women's Association
http://www.abwahq.org

This organization provides training, career management workshops, leadership development, and a support network for women in business professions.

CAREERS IN BUSINESS

Careers in Business
http://www.careers-in-business.com

This informative site, developed by business professionals, provides general information on a wide variety of business careers plus related online and print resources.

ACCOUNT COLLECTORS

ACA International
http://www.collector.com

Public site of the Association of Credit and Collection Professionals, an international trade association of credit and collection professionals. Learn about certification, collection and credit law, and legislation.

ACCOUNTING

Association of Latino Professionals in Finance and Accounting
http://www.alpfa.org

The Association of Latino Professionals in Finance and Accounting (ALPFA), formerly the American Association of Hispanic Certified Public Accountants (AAHCPA), was established in 1972 as the first national Latino professional association in the United States. The "Students" section provides programs and benefits to Latino students interested in accounting, finance, or related professions.

Careers in Accounting
http://www.careers-in-accounting.com

Learn about the skills and talents needed for a career in accounting, job options, links, and resources. Brought to you by *Careers in Business.com*.

Institute of Management Accountants
http://www.imanet.org

The Institute of Management Accountants (IMA) is an organization devoted exclusively to management accounting and financial management. Learn about certification requirements, career opportunities, and the benefits of student membership.

The Institute of Internal Auditors
http://www.theiia.org

Primarily geared towards professionals, this site contains sections on professional practices, code of ethics, standards, and the latest issues.

National Society of Accountants
http://www.nsacct.org

This is a professional organization for accounting and tax professionals. The Web site provides information and current issues concerning tax and accounting professionals, as well as member benefits and online journals.

ACTUARIAL SCIENCE

American Academy of Actuaries
http://www.actuary.org

Self proclaimed "...as the profession's voice on public policy and professionalism issues," the American Academy of Actuaries represents actuaries from all areas of practice. Visit "About Us" to find out what an actuary is.

Be An Actuary
http://www.beanactuary.org

Brought to you by the Casualty Actuarial Society (CAS), and the Society of Actuaries (SOA). Learn what an actuary is, what they do on the job, which schools to attend, and if you are suited for a career as an actuary. Separate sections for minority students, teachers, and parents. Excellent!

Casualty Actuarial Society
http://www.casact.org

This organization is the branch of actuarial science that deals with property and casualty.

Society of Actuaries
http://www.soa.org

Established in 1949, this organization hosts a variety of professional resources for actuaries.

BANKING

American Bankers Association
http://www.aba.com

Read about some of the issues in the world of banking.

Independent and Community Bankers of America
http://www.ibaa.org

This organization describes itself as the only national association dedicated to community banks.

ECONOMICS

American Economic Association
http://www.vanderbilt.edu/AEA

Established in 1885, this organization encourages economic research and nonpartisan economic discussion.

Association for Social Economics
http://www.socialeconomics.org

The Association for Social Economics was established in 1941. The purpose of this organization is to "...explore the ethical foundations and implications of economic analysis, along with the individual and social dimensions of economic problems, and to help shape economic policy that is consistent with the integral values of the person and a humane community."

Econometric Society
http://www.econometricsociety.org

Founded in 1930, the Econometric Society is an international society for the advancement of economic theory in its relation to statistics and mathematics.

National Association for Business Economics
http://www.nabe.com

Visit "Careers" for the latest edition of *Careers in Business Economics*. This free publication includes a collection of articles from *Business Economics*®, as well as information on education and training and results from their Salary Survey.

HEALTH CARE MANAGEMENT

American College of Healthcare Executives
http://www.ache.org

"Career Services" hosts a variety of career-related information and resources. Especially useful for beginning health care executives.

HUMAN RESOURCES

American Society for Training and Development
http://www.astd.org

The "Careers" section provides a wealth of information on salaries, advice from experts, and everything else you need to know about entering or moving up in the training profession.

National Association of Personnel Services
http://napsweb.org

Learn about the issues that affect the personnel and staffing industry.

National Human Resources Association
http://www.humanresources.org

An organization for the human resources management professional. Many services are for members only.

Society for Human Resource Management
http://www.shrm.org

The world's largest association devoted to human resource management.

INSURANCE

Insurance Institute of America
http://www.aicpcu.org

This site offers online courses, information about certification exams, and a variety of services for students, including a free educational survey to assist you in selecting appropriate courses.

Risk and Insurance Management Society, Inc.
http://www.rims.org

An organization for risk management professionals. Students should keep the "Career Center" in mind when they are ready to seek employment.

MBA

Do You See Yourself as an MBA?
http://mba.com

Find out if an MBA is right for you, learn about MBA careers, find a college program, and much more. A complete employment and career resource for MBAs.

National Black MBA Association
http://www.nbmbaa.org

An organization and support network for black MBA's.

MANAGEMENT

American Management Association
http://www.amanet.org

This site offers articles, e-learning, conferences, and resources.

MARKETING & ADVERTISING

American Advertising Federation
http://www.aaf.org

Members of this organization are comprised of advertisers, agencies, and media companies that comprise the nation's leading brands and corporations. Visit "College Connection" for college chapters, competitions, scholarships, internship opportunities, and career and industry resources.

American Association of Advertising Agencies
http://www.aaaa.org

This site offers news and information, upcoming events, publications, and initiatives.

American Marketing Association
http://www.marketingpower.com

This is the Web site of the American Marketing Association, a professional organization for marketing professionals. For career and salary information, visit the "Career Center."

Market Research Association
http://www.mra-net.org

An association for marketing research professionals. Visit the "Career & Training" section for more information about the opinion and market research industry.

Sales and Marketing Executives International
http://www.smei.org

Founded in 1935, SME-International is the worldwide association of sales and marketing management. The "Advancement" section offers career resources and certification information.

PURCHASING

American Purchasing Society
http://www.american-purchasing.com

The American Purchasing Society (APS) is a professional association of buyers and purchasing managers. Learn about certification and the job market.

National Association of Governmental Purchasing, Inc.
http://www.nigp.org

This organization provides its members with education, research, technical assistance, and networking opportunities in public purchasing.

National Association of Purchasing Management
http://www.ism.ws

This is the Web site of the Institute for Supply Management™ which was previously known as the National Association of Purchasing Management. Visit the "Career Center" for a variety of career resources.

REAL ESTATE & PROPERTY MANAGERS

Institute of Real Estate Management
http://www.irem.org

The Institute of Real Estate Management was founded in 1933 to educate, certify, and advocate for the real estate management industry.

International Council of Shopping Centers
http://www.icsc.org

Founded in 1957, the International Council of Shopping Centers (ICSC), is the global trade association of the shopping center industry. Publications, accreditation programs, job opportunities, and retail statistics.

National Association of Mortgage Brokers
http://www.namb.org

The National Association of Mortgage Brokers is a nonprofit, national association for the mortgage broker industry. They provide education, certification, and government affairs representation.

National Association of Residential Property Managers
http://www.narpm.org

Visit this Web site for information, certification, and issues affecting residential property owners.

RETAIL/SALES

National Association of Sales Professionals
http://www.nasp.com

Despite limited information, this site does provide descriptions of job openings, lists of potential employers, and industry links that may give prospective career seekers more information about the field.

National Retail Federation
http://www.nrf.com

The National Retail Federation (NRF) is the nation's largest retail trade association. For information on a career in retailing, select "NRF" then "Retail Careers."

Sales and Marketing Executives International
http://www.smei.org

Founded in 1935, SME-International is the worldwide association of sales and marketing management. The "Advancement" section offers career resources and certification information.

SECRETARIAL

American Society of Corporate Secretaries
http://www.ascs.org

The American Society of Corporate Secretaries is a professional association composed of corporate secretaries, assistant secretaries, and other persons involved with the functions of a corporate secretary.

International Association of Administrative Professionals
http://www.iaap-hq.org

An association for administrative support staff. Offers certification and membership information.

National Association of Legal Secretaries
http://www.nals.org

The National Association of Legal Secretaries was formed in 1929. Extensive information on education and career certification.

National Court Reporters Association
http://www.ncraonline.com

Information on the court reporting and captioning professions.

SECURITIES

The Securities Industry Association
http://www.sia.com

For information about career opportunities in the securities industry visit the "Career Resource Center."

INFORMATION TECHNOLOGY

Association for Information Technology Professionals
http://www.aitp.org

This site provides information on relevant issues and forums for networking with professional and student members throughout the United States.

Information Technology Association of America
http://www.itaa.org

This Web site provides information about the information technology industry, current issues, and links to other sites.

COMPUTER ENGINEERING (SEE ENGINEERING)

COMPUTER SCIENCE (SEE MATH & SCIENCE)

LIBRARY SCIENCE

American Association of Law Libraries
http://www.aallnet.org

Learn about a career in law librarianship at this Web site. Choose "Education & Careers" for information about schools, educational requirements, and careers.

American Library Association
http://www.ala.org

This site features news, events, and FAQ's.

Association of Research Libraries
http://arl.cni.org

Choose "Services," then "Career Resources," for an article under "Related ARL Resources" on careers in research libraries and information science.

Medical Library Association
http://www.mlanet.org

An association for the health information professional.

Special Libraries Association
http://www.sla.org

This is the international association for information resource experts, or special librarians, that work in corporate, academic, and government settings.

CHAPTER 12

Engineering and Industrial Web Sites

THE ENGINEERING AND INDUSTRIAL CAREER CLUSTER

The Engineering and Industrial career cluster includes occupations concerned with the design and construction of buildings, equipment, highways, roads, utilization of land, and processing systems. People in these occupations often have interests and skills in *data*, *ideas*, and/or *things*. These occupations require technical skills and a high aptitude in mathematics, creative thinking, and problem solving.

People who work in the manufacturing, trade, and transportation fields often value reliability and practicality. They often enjoy manual and mechanical activities, such as using machines, tools, and objects.

Construction and extraction occupations involve working on materials at a specific site, which will change over time. People in these occupations usually have interests and skills in *things* and use a variety of tools to perform their duties. They must have a certain degree of physical strength in some of the occupations and mechanical aptitude specific to their occupation. Most have to effectively manage their time, materials, and resources to meet construction deadlines.

Transportation occupations involve operating and controlling equipment used to move people and/or materials. People in these occupations usually have interests and skills in *things*. They have the mechanical aptitude to operate the various modes of transportation and perform minor repairs. They must manage their time and materials effectively to keep their equipment operable.

ENGINEERING

American Society for Engineering Education
http://www.asee.org

The "Engineering K–12 Center" section is designed for high school students interested in engineering and engineering technology. This section contains everything you ever wanted to know about the field of engineering. Select "Students" to learn about the benefits of being an engineer, different disciplines, famous people, and schools. You can even complete a self-assessment to determine if an engineering career fits your interests and lifestyle.

WOMEN, MINORITIES, AND STUDENTS

American Indian Science & Engineering Society
http://www.aises.org

This national, nonprofit organization bridges science and technology with traditional native values.

Junior Engineering Technical Society, Inc
http://www.jets.org

The JETS organization promotes an interest in engineering, science, mathematics, and technology, and provides real-world engineering and problem-solving experiences to high school students through contests and education.

National Society of Black Engineers
http://www.nsbe.org

This organization is managed by African-American engineering students.

National Society of Professional Engineers
http://www.nspe.org

The organization for licensed, professional engineers.

Society of Hispanic Professional Engineers
http://www.shpe.org

An organization for Hispanic professional engineers.

Society of Women Engineers
http://www.swe.org

This organization promotes the role of women in engineering. Offers student services such as scholarships and career advice. Student chapters are active at most colleges and universities.

Women Tech World
http://www.womentechworld.org

An online place for women technicians to connect with each other. Career biographies and stories.

Women's Engineering Society
http://www.wes.org.uk

Homepage of the Women's Engineering Society based in the United Kingdom.

AEROSPACE ENGINEERING

American Institute of Aeronautics and Astronautics
http://www.aiaa.org

The American Institute of Aeronautics and Astronautics (AIAA) is the principal society of the aerospace engineer and scientist. Select "Students & Educators," then "Ask An Engineer" for information about careers in aerospace engineering.

Careers in Aerospace
http://www.nasa.gov

Visit this site if you're interested in a career in aerospace. Select "Students" to learn about career oppoptunities in aerospace. Also includes related NASA Internet links.

Women of NASA
http://quest.arc.nasa.gov/women/intro.html

This educational site highlights the contribution of women in NASA's development.

AGRICULTURAL ENGINEERING

American Society of Agricultural Engineers
http://www.asae.org

The society for engineering in agriculture, food, and biological systems.

ARCHITECTURAL ENGINEERING

The Architectural Engineering Institute
http://www.aeinstitute.org

Established in 1998, the Architectural Engineering Institute (AEI) is an institute within the American Society of Civil Engineers. Visit "FAQ" to learn what an architectural engineer does.

BIOMEDICAL ENGINEERING

The American Institute for Medical and Biological Engineering
http://www.aimbe.org

This is the professional organization for the fields of medical and biological engineering.

Biomedical Engineering Society
http://www.bmes.org

The Biomedical Engineering Society represents individuals in both the biomedical and engineering fields. Learn what a biomedical engineer does by reading *Planning a Career in Biomedical Engineering,* located in the "Careers" section.

Institute of Biomedical Science
http://www.ibms.org

The Institute of Biomedical Science is the professional body for biomedical scientists in all fields of work, including medical laboratory scientific officers in the National Health Service and related services in the United Kingdom and Ireland. To learn what a biomedical scientist is and the career opportunities available, visit the "Science" section.

CHEMICAL ENGINEERING

American Chemical Society
http://www.acs.org

The professional organization of chemistry professionals. The "Professionals" section offers career and job information and links to other resources.

American Institute of Chemical Engineers
http://www.aiche.org

Web site of the professional organization for chemical engineers. Click on "Careers & Employment" for career-related links for students. "Students & Young Engineers" has information and resources for engineering students.

CIVIL ENGINEERING

Air & Waste Management Association
http://www.awma.org

Founded in 1907 by Canadian and American smoke inspectors, this organization's membership includes scientists, engineers, policymakers, attorneys, and consultants. The "Education" section contains a list of colleges and universities offering undergraduate and advanced degrees in the environmental profession.

American Academy of Environmental Engineers
http://www.aaee.net

To learn about the field of environmental engineering, select "About AAEE," then "Careers."

American Society of Civil Engineers
http://www.asce.org

The American Society of Civil Engineers has been providing information to professionals and academics in civil engineering for 150 years. This site features news, professional issues, and publications. Click on "Kids & Careers" for career information.

COMPUTER ENGINEERING

IEEE Computer Society
http://computer.org

Select the "Career Services Center" for information about careers in computer science and computer engineering. Information on student membership, scholarships, contests, and links to related engineering sites.

Institute of Electrical and Electronic Engineers
http://www.ieee.org

Through its membership, IEEE is a leading authority in technical areas ranging from computer engineering, biomedical technology, and telecommunications, to electric power, aerospace, and consumer electronics, among others. Visit the "Careers & Education" section for career and employment resources. Includes sections for students and women.

Association for Information Technology Professionals
http://www.aitp.org

This site provides career information and activities via a network of over 300 college and university student chapters located throughout the United States and Canada.

Institute for Certification of Computing Professionals
http://www.iccp.org

It is the world's leading certification body for information and communications technology (ICT) professionals. To learn about the benefits of certification in this field first select "Find out more...," then "Frequently Asked Questions."

COMPUTER SCIENCE (SEE MATH AND SCIENCE)

DRAFTING

American Design Drafting Association
http://www.adda.org

The premier organization for designers, drafters, architects, illustrators, and technical artists.

ELECTRICAL ENGINEERING

Institute of Electrical and Electronic Engineers
http://www.ieee.org

Through its membership, IEEE is a leading authority in technical areas ranging from computer engineering, biomedical technology and telecommunications, to electric power, aerospace and consumer electronics, among others. Visit the "Careers & Education" section for career and employment resources. Includes sections for students and women.

IEEE Computer Society
http://computer.org

The "Career Services Center" contains information about careers in computer science and computer engineering. This site also provides information on student membership, scholarships, contests, and links to related engineering sites.

ENVIRONMENTAL ENGINEERING
(SEE CIVIL ENGINEERING)

INDUSTRIAL ENGINEERING

Institute of Industrial Engineers
http://www.iienet.org

Visit the "Student Center" for information about student chapters, scholarships, and accredited programs. The IIE "Career Resources" page can be accessed either through the "Student Center" or the "Career Center" section. It contains articles about choosing a career in industrial engineering, and career options.

MATERIALS ENGINEERING

ASM International, A Society for Materials Engineers
http://www.asm-intl.org

ASM International is the society for materials engineers and scientists. The "Career Center" has information on careers, employment, salary, and scholarships.

Materials Research Society
http://www.mrs.org

This colorful site features an online membership directory, news, meeting information, and an electronic library.

Minerals, Metals, and Materials
http://www.tms.org

This Web site seeks to promote the global science and engineering professions concerned with minerals, metals, and materials. Select "Student Members" to view the TMS Student Members homepage. "Continuing Education" includes information on professional registration, and the "Career Resource Center" answers commonly asked questions about career opportunities in materials science and engineering.

MECHANICAL ENGINEERING

American Society of Mechanical Engineers
http://www.asme.org

ASME was founded in 1880 as the American Society of Mechanical Engineers. Today ASME International is a nonprofit educational and technical organization serving a worldwide membership of 125,000. Visit the "Career Center" for employment and salary information as well as other career resources.

NUCLEAR ENGINEERING

American Nuclear Society
http://www.ans.org

This site contains standards, publications, press releases, and nuclear links.

SURVEYING

American Congress on Surveying and Mapping
http://www.acsm.net

Originally named the National Congress on Surveying and Mapping when it was founded in June 1941, the name changed to encompass members from Canada and South America. Visit the "For Students Only" section for information about careers in surveying.

American Society for Photogrammetry and Remote Sensing
http://www.asprs.org

To find out what a photogrammetrist is, visit "About the Society."

Bureau of Land Management
http://www.blm.gov

From the U.S. Department of the Interior. Read about what a job with the BLM would entail by choosing "What We Do."

Federal Geographic Data Committee
http://fgdc.er.usgs.gov/fgdc.html

The Federal Geographic Data Committee coordinates the development of the National Spatial Data Infrastructure (NSDI). The NSDI encompasses policies, standards, and procedures for organizations to cooperatively produce and share geographic data. The 17 federal agencies that make up the FGDC are developing the NSDI in cooperation with organizations from state, local, and tribal governments, the academic community, and the private sector.

FIG
http://www.fig.net

This is the Web site of the International Federation of Surveyors (FIG).

International Society for Photogrammetry and Remote Sensing
http://www.isprs.org

Select "Links," then "Education & Tutorials" for publications, software, tutorials, and other information that will enable you to see what the fields of photogrammetry and remote sensing are all about.

Land Surveyor's Reference Page
http://www.lsrp.com

This Web site is a collection of links to every aspect of the land surveying profession.

Penn State Surveying Program
http://surveying.wb.psu.edu

To discover all of the exciting and diverse opportunities within the surveying profession, visit "More Information" and "Career Opportunities." Also includes a comprehensive resource of links to other surveying-related organizations, journals, companies, and job search resources.

Topographic Engineering Center
http://www.tec.army.mil

Learn what this branch of the U.S. Army Corps of Engineers does. Courtesy of the U.S. Army Corp. of Engineers.

U.S. Coast Survey
http://chartmaker.ncd.noaa.gov

The Office of Coast Survey is known for its navigational products. Visit "Hydrographic Surveys" and "Research and Development" for descriptions of the hydrographic surveying and cartography fields within the surveying profession.

U.S. Geological Survey
http://www.usgs.gov

The USGS is the nation's largest water, earth, and biological science and civilian mapping agency. Select "About USGS," then "Ask Us" for educational resources and information about a variety of geological and environmental topics.

Urban & Regional Information Systems Association
http://www.urisa.org

The Urban and Regional Information Systems Association (URISA) is considered the premier organization for professionals using Geographic Information Systems (GIS) and other information technologies to solve challenges in all state and local government agencies and departments. Visit the "GIS & IT Career Center" for salary information, job descriptions, and links to colleges and universities with GIS programs.

BUILDING & TRADE

CARPENTRY

Associated General Contractors of America
http://www.agc.org

Associated General Contractors is the nation's largest and oldest construction trade association. It was established in 1918 at the request of President Woodrow Wilson.

National Association of Home Builders
http://www.nahb.org

This is the new Web site of the National Association of Home Builders (NAHB), formerly www.nahb.com. NAHB is a federation of more than 800 state and local builders' associations throughout the United States. Contains information and articles on various building and housing issues.

CONCRETE AND TERRAZZO

National Concrete Masonry Association
http://www.ncma.org

Established in 1918, the National Concrete Masonry Association (NCMA) is the national trade association that represents the concrete masonry industry.

National Terrazzo and Mosaic Association
http://www.ntma.com

The National Terrazzo and Mosaic Association, Inc. is a full service nonprofit trade association. The association establishes national standards for all terrazzo floor and wall systems. Information on terrazzo and its application.

DRYWALL AND CEILING TILE

Ceilings and Interior Systems Construction Association
http://www.cisca.org

This is a new Web site featuring news, conventions, and events.

ELECTRICIANS

Independent Electrical Contractors
http://www.ieci.org

This organization is the online resource for the electrical industry. Choose "Apprenticeship" for opportunities in this area.

National Electrical Contractors Association
http://www.necanet.org

This site provides a variety of information for those interested in electrical construction.

INSULATION

National Insulation Association
http://www.insulation.org

This organization represents the mechanical and specialty insulation industry. Select "Careers" for industry-specific information.

GLAZIERS

Glass Association of North America
http://www.glasswebsite.com

Information about the glass industry.

MASONRY

The Masonry Society
http://www.masonrysociety.org

The Masonry Society is an international group of people interested in the art and science of masonry.

The National Concrete Masonry Association
http://www.ncma.org

Established in 1918, the National Concrete Masonry Association (NCMA) is the national trade association that represents the concrete masonry industry.

PAINTERS

International Union of Painters and Allied Trades
http://www.ibpat.org

The International Union of Painters and Allied Trades claims to be one of the fastest growing labor unions in North America. For information on how to enter the profession, first select "Links" at the top of the page, then "Education, Training, and Apprenticeship."

PIPELAYERS

United Association of Journeymen and Apprentices of the Plumbing and Pipefitting Industry
http://ua.org

United Association of Journeymen and Apprentices of the Plumbing and Pipefitting Industry of the United States and Canada (UA) is a multi-craft union whose members are engaged in the fabrication, installation, and servicing of piping systems.

PLUMBING, HEATING & COOLING

Plumbing-Heating-Cooling Contractors Association
http://www.phccweb.org

As the oldest trade organization in the construction industry, PHCC has been an advocate for plumbing, heating, and cooling contractors since 1883. Visit "Gateway to PHC Industry" for a comprehensive list of links to related construction associations.

STRUCTURAL IRON & STEEL

Iron and Steel Society
http://www.iss.org

In addition to a variety of services for members, this site also features articles, member information, student scholarships, and a job recruitment program. Students should keep the this site in mind when they're ready to graduate. Also available in Spanish.

MANUFACTURING

American Welding Society
http://www.aws.org

Read about the latest technology and innovations in the welding industry. For career and education information, visit "Services" at the top of the page.

Hard Hatted Women
http://www.hardhattedwomen.org

This organization began in 1979 when three women—a telephone repair technician, a steelworker, and a truck driver—formed a support group for trades women. Check out the "Career Corner" for honest depictions of various trade occupations, work conditions, and salaries.

MACHINING

Iron and Steel Society
http://www.iss.org

In addition to a variety of services for members, this site also features articles, member information, student scholarships, and a job recruitment program. Students should keep this site in mind when they're ready to graduate. Also available in Spanish.

National Tooling and Machinery Association
http://www.ntma.org

The National Tooling and Machining Association is the representative of the precision custom manufacturing industry in the United States.

Precision Machined Products Association
http://www.pmpa.org

Visit "About the PMPA & the Industry" to learn all about the precision machined products industry and the products they manufacture. This site also provides some excellent information about career opportunities, which can be accessed through "Career Information."

Precision Metalforming Association, Tool and Die Division
http://www.metalforming.com

Visit the "Educational Foundation" for in-depth information about metal forming careers including everyday products, industry tours, training, salary, and career opportunities.

TRANSPORTATION & LOGISTICS

AIR TRAFFIC CONTROLLERS

National Air Traffic Controllers Association
http://www.natca.org

To find out more about a career as an air traffic controller select "About NATCA," then "Career Info."

International Federation of Air Traffic
Controllers' Associations
http://www.ifatca.org

IFATCA is the nonpolitical and nonindustrial world professional organization representing approximately 40,000 air traffic controllers in more than 100 countries. "Links" contains related aviation Web sites and resources.

AVIATION

Aircraft Owners and Pilots Association
http://www.aopa.org

An active organization that features a variety of aviation information and resources. "Learn to Fly" provides information, articles, and biographies about people who fly.

Airline Pilots Association International
http://www.alpa.org

The ALPA represents pilots in the U.S. and Canada. News releases, an e-zine, list of job opportunities, and reports on air safety are included in this Web site.

Air Transport Association
http://www.airlines.org

The ATA is the only trade organization for the principal United States airlines. This site provides industry information, news, and publications. To read about the history of aviation, select "About Us," then "Airlines 101."

Careers in Aviation and Aerodynamics
http://wings.avkids.com

The K–8 Aeronautics Internet Textbook. The "Careers" section describes careers in aviation. Hosted by the National Business Aviation Association.

Federal Aviation Administration
http://www.faa.gov

This is the homepage of the government regulatory body for the aviation industry. Includes information on airline safety and accident investigations.

Flying History
http://www.flyinghistory.com

Flying History features books, a photo gallery, and various resources about the history of flight in the past hundred years.

International Civil Aviation Organization
http://www.icao.int

Career-related information can be found under "FAQ."

National Business Aviation Association
http://www.nbaa.org

This association is concerned with the interests of companies that own or operate aircraft. Business aviation issues, government affairs, and education sections.

Women in Aviation
http://www.women-in-aviation.com

This Web site features a large collection of educational, historical, and networking resources for women in all aspects of aviation.

FLIGHT ATTENDANTS

Association of Flight Attendants
http://www.afanet.org

This is the Web site of the Association of Flight Attendants (AFA), the world's largest labor union organized by flight attendants for flight attendants.

CHAPTER 13

Health and Health Care Web Sites

THE HEALTH AND HEALTH CARE CAREER CLUSTER

Health care practitioners and technical occupations. This cluster includes occupations dealing with the prevention and diagnosis of human and animal ailments, and prescribes medical and surgical treatments. People in these occupations often have interests and skills in *people* and *data*, and value helping others in a medical setting. They have aptitudes in acquiring and evaluating information, and also must interpret and communicate information effectively to others. Good problem-solving and decision-making skills are also necessary.

COUNSELING & PSYCHOLOGY

ART THERAPY

The American Art Therapy Association
http://www.arttherapy.org

This is a nonprofit organization for professionals and students in art therapy. Visit "About Art Therapy" for an overview of the profession.

COUNSELING

American Counseling Association
http://www.counseling.org

The professional organization for counselors. The "Student" section contains information about the counseling profession, its specialty areas, and various issues like "Choosing a Graduate Program."

National Rehabilitation Counseling Association
http://nrca-net.org

To find out what a rehabilitation counselor does, select "Professional Development," then "Scope of Practice."

American School Counselor Association
http://www.schoolcounselor.org

This is the professional organization for secondary school counselors. Visit "Careers/Roles" to learn what a school counselor does.

MUSIC THERAPY

American Music Therapy Association
http://www.musictherapy.org

Visit "Careers" for information on a careers, schools, personal qualifications, and job opportunities in music therapy.

PSYCHOLOGY

American Psychological Association
http://www.apa.org

This Web site is the professional organization for psychologists. Articles, code of ethics, how to find a psychologist, and much more. Visit "Students" for career-related information.

Association for the Advancement of Applied Sport Psychology
http://www.aaasponline.org

The "What is Applied Sport Psychology?" section contains a wealth of information about the field of sport psychology.

Association of Black Psychologists
http://www.abpsi.org

An organization for African-American psychologists.

The Association for Women in Psychology
http://www.awpsych.org

This organization is committed to encouraging feminist psychological research, theory, and activism.

National Association of School Psychologists
http://www.nasponline.org

In addition to information about the professional organization, students can obtain free brochures and career information about becoming a school psychologist.

SOCIAL WORK (SEE HUMAN SERVICES)

HEALTH & HEALTH CARE

ATHLETIC COACHES

National High School Athletic Coaches Association
http://www.hscoaches.org

This association was created in 1965 by coaches, for coaches. News, information, photos, and job openings.

ATHLETIC TRAINER

National Athletic Trainers' Association
http://www.nata.org

Browse through this Web site for articles, news, and information on issues and topics in the athletic training profession. A salary survey and a list of accredited programs can be found under "ATC Employment."

CHIROPRACTIC

American Chiropractic Association
http://www.amerchiro.org

The American Chiropractic Association (ACA) is the largest professional association in the world representing doctors of chiropractic. "About ACA" contains the "Student ACA" section, which has information on student chapters, educational requirements, and careers.

International Chiropractors Association
http://www.chiropractic.org

This is the oldest international chiropractic organization in the world. Select "Chiropractic Information" for quick facts, career information, and health articles.

CLINICAL LABORATORY SCIENCE

American Society for Clinical Laboratory Science
http://www.ascls.org

Visit the "Career Center" for career information about clinical laboratory science.

DENTAL

American Dental Assistants Association
http://www.dentalassistant.org

Read "About Us" for an overview of the dental assisting profession.

American Dental Society
http://www.ada.org

The professional organization for dental health professionals. Visit "Dental Professionals" to locate the "Education" section for an extensive resource of career-related information including career brochures and fact sheets for dentistry, dental hygiene, dental assisting, and dental laboratory technology.

Hispanic Dental Association
http://www.hdassoc.org

This Web site promotes and supports Hispanic dental practitioners. There is a section for students, as well as information on scholarship programs.

National Association of Dental Laboratories
http://www.nadl.org

Learn about dental technology certification in this Web site. Visit "Links & Resources" for an extensive list of dental Web sites.

EMTs AND PARAMEDICS

American Ambulance Association
http://www.the-aaa.org

Read about issues, policies, and other events that concern the ambulance services industry. Visit "Links" for a Web list of other protective service organizations.

National Association of Emergency Medical Technicians
http://www.naemt.org

A comprehensive Web site provided as a service to the EMS community by the National Association of Emergency Medical Technicians. View this site for related links, current events, history, the EMT oath, code of ethics, and membership news.

HOLISTIC

American Holistic Health Association
http://ahha.org

Learn about holistic health by browsing this informative Web site.

MASSAGE THERAPY

American Massage Therapy Association
http://amtamassage.org

Visit "Students" to learn about career opportunities and training in massage therapy.

Career At Your Fingertips
http://www.careeratyourfingertips.com

A resource for people thinking about becoming a massage professional. FAQ's, forms of body work, licensing laws, and a school directory are included. Features *Massage: A Career at Your Fingertips* by Martin Ashley.

MEDICINE (PHYSICIANS & DOCTORS)

American College of Sports Medicine
http://www.acsm.org

A large part of this organization's mission is devoted to public awareness and education about the positive aspects of physical activity.

American Medical Association
http://www.ama-assn.org

The professional organization for the medical community.

The American Medical Women's Association
http://www.amwa-doc.org

Learn about topics and issues affecting women's health and women in the medical profession.

Association of American Medical Colleges
http://www.aamc.org

Visit "Popular Links" for insightful information about careers in medicine and "Medical Schools" for information on how to apply to medical school.

National Academy of Sciences
http://www.nas.edu

The National Academy of Sciences advise the government on scientific and technical matters. Read online reports, projects, and publications.

MEDICAL ASSISTANT

American Association of Medical Assistants
http://www.aama-ntl.org

For information about being a medical assistant and accredited programs, visit "Medical Assisting & CMAs" and "Become a CMA."

NURSING

American Nurses Association
http://www.nursingworld.org

A full-service professional organization representing registered nurses. News and announcements, workplace issues, and an online journal, *Issues in Nursing*.

The National League of Nursing
http://www.nln.org

Among other things, this organization offers scholarships, training, research grants, and professional development.

NUTRITION

American Dietetic Association
http://www.eatright.org

Select "Careers and Students" for information about becoming a registered dietitian, answers to frequently asked questions, and a list of accredited programs.

OCCUPATIONAL THERAPY

American Occupational Therapy Association
http://www.aota.org

The professional organization for occupational therapists. Visit "Students" for career and educational information.

OPTOMETRY

American Optometric Association
http://www.aoanet.org

Select "About AOA" to find out what a doctor of optometry is. Also visit "Eye Conditions and Concerns," and "Clinical Care" to learn more about the field of optometry.

PHARMACY

American College of Clinical Pharmacy
http://www.accp.com

To learn about board certification and career planning, visit "Career Development."

American Association of Pharmaceutical Scientists
http://www.aaps.org

Career-related information can be found in the "Career Network" section. "Students/Student Center" includes a listing of graduate and undergraduate schools of pharmacy, and contains information on career opportunities in the pharmaceutical sciences.

American Pharmacists Association
http://www.aphanet.org

Founded in 1852, this society was the first professional association of pharmacists established in the United States. For information on student chapters and additional information about the profession, select "Academies & Interest Groups," and then "Student Pharmacists."

PHYSICAL THERAPY

Physical Therapy Association
http://www.apta.org

The "Jobs/Career Center" section contains information about choosing physical therapy as a career.

PHYSICIAN ASSISTANT

American Academy of Physician Assistants
http://www.aapa.org

This organization represents physician assistants (PAs) in all specialties and all employment settings. Read about professional issues and licensing requirements.

Student Academy of the American Academy of
Physician Assistants
http://www.saaapa.aapa.org

This organization functions as an information resource for PA students, as well as those interested in exploring a career as a physician assistant. To learn about a career as a PA, go to the "Pre-PA Students" section.

PODIATRY

American Podiatric Medical Association
http://www.apma.org

To learn about careers in podiatry, visit "Careers in Podiatric Medicine." To learn about feet and foot disorders, select "Foot Health."

RADIOLOGIC TECHNOLOGISTS

American Society of Radiologic Technologists
http://www.asrt.org

Visit "The Public" to learn about the field of radiologic technology. The "Career Center" contains wage and salary information.

RESPIRATORY THERAPY

American Association for Respiratory Care
http://www.aarc.org

Visit the "Career" section if you are thinking about a career in respiratory therapy. "Education" includes a list of accredited respiratory care programs in the United States.

SPEECH-LANGUAGE PATHOLOGY & AUDIOLOGY

Acoustical Society of America
http://asa.aip.org

This organization is concerned with acoustics and its applications. Career information can be accessed by selecting "Resources," then "Education."

American Speech-Language-Hearing Association
http://www.asha.org

The professional organization for speech and language pathologists and audiologists. Visit "For Students" for career information on communication sciences and disorders.

SPORTS MEDICINE (SEE MEDICINE)

SPORTS PSYCHOLOGY (SEE PSYCHOLOGY)

SURGICAL TECHNOLOGISTS

Association of Surgical Technologists
http://www.ast.org

This Web site provides information on surgical technology professions, educational programs, legislative policy, and news.

THERAPEUTIC RECREATION THERAPY

American Association for Leisure and Recreation
http://www.aalr.org

This is the homepage of the American Association for Leisure and Recreation, which is an organization for recreation professionals.

The American Alliance for Health, Physical Education, Recreation, and Dance
http://www.aahperd.org

Visit this Web site to learn more about program accreditation, areas of interest within this field, and related associations.

American Therapeutic Recreation Association
http://www.atra-tr.org

The *American Therapeutic Recreation Association (ATRA)* is the largest national organization representing the interests and needs of recreational therapists. Visit "Education & Careers" and "Students" for career information.

National Recreation & Park Association
http://www.nrpa.org

Visit "Education/Training" to learn about educational and career opportunities.

CHAPTER 14

Human Services Web Sites

THE HUMAN SERVICES CAREER CLUSTER

Human services occupations are concerned with the needs of people and their communities, families, and spiritual development. They primarily have interests and skills in *people* and resolving personal and societal issues. People in these occupations value helping others and have high interpersonal skills. They are friendly, trusting, warm, enjoy working with others, and prefer team approaches.

People in education and training occupations have direct contact with individuals in an educational setting. People in these occupations generally have interests and skills in *people* and value helping others to learn and develop. Their skills include speaking, listening, teaching, and serving others.

EDUCATION & TRAINING

Careers in Teaching
http://www.gradlink.edu.au

To read about careers in teaching, select "Industry Career Profiles" under "What Job for You." The complete copy is downloadable. An excellent source of information for anyone interested in teaching.

National Commission on Teaching & America's Future
http://www.nctaf.org

For a complete list of professional teaching organizations in any subject, visit "Related Links."

National Education Association
http://www.nea.org

The national association for educators. Student members receive a monthly newsletter and an annual magazine that covers job issues and student concerns.

BIOLOGY TEACHER

National Association of Biology Teachers
http://www.nabt.org

Offers a bulletin board and "Ask an Expert" section.

DANCE TEACHER

National Dance Teachers Association
http://www.ndta.org.uk

Visit "Careers in Dance" for information on the wide variety of jobs that are connected to dance in some way, including teaching. A United Kingdom Web site.

ENGLISH TEACHER

National Council of Teachers of English
http://www.ncte.org

Online resources, issues, and articles.

GERMAN TEACHER

American Association of Teachers of German
http://www.aatg.org

Professional development, materials, and Web resources for German language teachers.

HISTORY TEACHER

Society for History Education
http://www.csulb.edu/~histeach

Devoted to teaching history in secondary and higher education.

MATHEMATICS TEACHER

National Council of Teachers of Mathematics
http://www.nctm.org

A national association serving mathematics teachers.

MUSIC TEACHER

Music Teachers National Association
http://www.mtna.org

An organization for music teaching professionals. Learn about certification and events.

National Association of Teachers of Singing
http://www.nats.org

A nonprofit organization for teachers of vocal education. Offers a voice competition, an art song composition award, intern programs, and online journals.

PHYSICS TEACHER

American Association of Physics Teachers
http://www.aapt.org

An organization for physics teachers at the high school and college level.

PRINCIPAL

National Association of Secondary School Principals
http://www.nassp.org

Read about events, student activities, resources, and other issues concerning middle and high school principals.

READING TEACHER

International Reading Association
http://www.reading.org

This organization is dedicated to promoting a high level of literacy. Also contains literacy links and a list of graduate programs in reading.

SCHOOL COUNSELOR (SEE COUNSELING)

SCIENCE TEACHER

National Science Teachers Organization
http://www.nsta.org/

Professional organization for people interested in teaching science. To find out if a career as a science teacher is right for you, select "Other Visitors," then "Students."

SOCIAL STUDIES TEACHER

National Council for the Social Studies
http://www.ncss.org

Visit this Web site for news, legislative updates, awards, resources, and career opportunities.

SPECIAL EDUCATION

American Sign Language Teachers Association
http://www.aslta.org

ASLTA is an organization of more than 1,000 ASL and deaf studies educators from elementary through graduate education.

Council for Exceptional Children
http://www.cec.sped.org

An international organization promoting the educational outcomes of exceptional children. Issues, public policy, and upcoming events.

National Clearinghouse for Professions in
Special Education
http://www.special-ed-careers.org

This Web site is made possible through a cooperative agreement between the National Clearinghouse on Careers and Professions Related to Early Intervention and Education for Children with Disabilities, the U.S. Department of Education, the Office of Special

Education Programs, and the Council for Exceptional Children. This site offers career information, educator resources, a research library, and recruitment services. Learn about what special educators do in the "Career Choices in Special Education" section.

HUMAN SERVICES

CHILD CARE

National Child Care Association
http://www.nccanet.org

This national association serves the private, licensed childhood care and education community. Certification, legislative updates, news, and events.

National Association for Family Child Care
http://www.nafcc.org

The mission of NAFCC is to support the profession of family child care and to promote high quality, family child care through accreditation, leadership training, technical assistance, public education, and policy initiatives.

FUNERAL DIRECTORS

American Board of Funeral Service Education
http://www.abfse.org

This is the national academic accreditation agency for college and university programs in funeral service and mortuary science Education. Select "FAQs" for career information and "Scholarship" for information about their scholarship program.

National Funeral Directors Association
http://www.nfda.org

Visit the "About Funeral Service" page for general information about the funeral service profession, as well as trends and statistics related to the industry.

SOCIAL WORK

The National Association of Social Workers
http://www.naswdc.org

To learn more about the practical applications of social work, visit
"Professional Development," and then select "Specialty Practice
Sections."

GOVERNMENT & PUBLIC ADMINISTRATION

HISTORY

American Historical Association
http://www.theaha.org

This is a professional organization for historians. The "Jobs & Careers"
section contains some interesting articles such as *"What Can You Do
With an Undergraduate Degree in History?"*

American Association for State and Local History
http://www.aaslh.org

Learn about issues and topics of interest to professionals who are interested in preserving and interpreting state and local history.

World History Association
www.thewha.org

The mission of the World History Association (WHA) is to promote
the study of global history. Competitions, publications, and resources
are also included in this Web site.

URBAN & REGIONAL PLANNING

American Planning Association
http://www.planning.org

Learn about the broad field of urban and regional planning by exploring this web site. Visit "Jobs & Careers" for specific career information.

Urban and Regional Information Systems Association
http://www.urisa.org

The Urban and Regional Information Systems Association (URISA) is considered the premier organization for professionals using Geographic Information Systems (GIS) and other information technologies to solve challenges in all state and local government agencies and departments. Visit the "GIS & IT Career Center" for salary information, job descriptions, and links to colleges and universities with GIS programs.

HOSPITALITY & TOURISM

CULINARY

American Culinary Federation
http://www.acfchefs.org

This is the professional chef's organization. For information on certification and apprenticeships, select "Education." The "Find" section contains a searchable database enabling users to locate programs, judges, and local chapters all across the United States.

International Association of Hotel, Restaurant, and Institutional Education
http://www.chrie.org

Check out college programs and scholarship opportunities in the "Just for Students" section.

National Restaurant Association
http://www.restaurant.org

Learn about the restaurant industry in this Web site. Click on "Careers & Education" for career-specific information, employment, and education and training opportunities.

Society for Food Service Management
http://www.sfm-online.org

This organization is geared toward executives in the on-site food service industry. Visit "Links" for a list of Web links to a variety of food service-related topics of interest.

Women Chefs and Restaurateurs
http://www.womenchefs.org

The purpose of this Web site is to promote the education and advancement of women in the restaurant industry.

HOTEL & RESTAURANT

American Hotel & Lodging Association
http://www.ahma.com

This site contains current events, governmental affairs, and other news of interest to individuals in the hotel and lodging industry.

TRAVEL AGENTS

American Society of Travel Agents
http://www.astanet.com

For educational programs, scholarships, information on becoming a travel agent, and job opportunities, visit "Education & Careers."

The Travel Institute
http://www.icta.com

The Travel Institute is an international, nonprofit organization that educates and certifies travel industry professionals at all stages of their career. Although this site is primarily concerned with offering training programs, there is a variety of information on certification, and a list of licensed schools that can be located by state.

LAW & PUBLIC SAFETY

COURT REPORTERS

National Court Reporters Association
http://www.ncraonline.com

Information on the court reporting and captioning professions.

CRIMINAL JUSTICE

Academy of Criminal Justice Sciences
http://www.acjs.org

Established in 1963, this international organization promotes criminal justice education, research, and policy analysis. Visit "Resources" to do a search for criminal justice schools.

Careers in Criminal Justice
http://www.dccced.edu/cvc/director/la/cj/ccjinto.htm

Read about careers in Corrections, Forensic Science, Law Enforcement, Private Security and the Courts. Courtesy of Cedar Valley College.

Federal Law Enforcement Careers
http://www.policeemployment.com

This web site contains descriptions of law enforcement jobs with the federal government.

National Institute of Correction
http://www.nicic.org

Learn about training opportunities, issues, and in-depth articles and descriptions of specialty areas in the field of corrections. Courtesy of the U.S. Department of Justice.

FIREFIGHTERS

National Fire Academy
http://www.usfa.fema.gov

Brought to you by the Federal Emergency Management Agency. This site contains resources and articles on every area of fire safety.

National Fire Protection Association
http://www.nfpa.org

Founded in 1896, the National Fire Protection Association has a Web site that offers articles, news releases, and a wide variety of professional resources. Visit the "Public Education" section for educational resources, including a booklet detailing the Fire Inspector Certification Program.

FORENSIC SCIENCE

American Society of Crime Laboratory Directors
http://www.ascld.org

This Web site provides a list of forensic-related links, as well as information for students on scholarships and careers.

Young Forensic Scientists Forum
http://www.aafs.org/yfsf/

The Young Forensic Scientists Forum (YFSF) is a group within the American Academy of Forensic Sciences (AAFS). The Web site provides resource links to professional associations, as well as career and educational information.

INVESTIGATORS

Council of International Investigators
http://www.cii2.org

This informative Web site features a public forum and a chat room. Select "About CII," then "Areas of Expertise" for a list of specialty areas within the investigation field.

International Association of Arson Investigators
http://www.firearson.com

Stay up-to-date on the arson investigation industry with news, events, and articles.

National Association of Legal Investigators
http://www.nalionline.org

This organization was formed for professional legal investigators who are actively engaged in negligence investigations. For a description of what a legal investigator does and the certification requirements, select "NALI Certified Legal Investigator."

LAW

American Bar Association
http://www.abanet.org

Legal and professional resources, governmental advocacy, and resources for law students.

Women's Bar Association
http://www.wbadc.org

Information and education for women attorneys, lawyers, and judges.

PARALEGAL

American Association for Paralegal Education
http://www.aafpe.org

Information on how to find a paralegal program in your area.

National Association of Legal Assistants
http://www.nala.org

This site provides continuing education and professional development for paralegals and legal assistants.

National Federation of Paralegal Associations
http://www.paralegals.org

This Web site contains helpful information about the paralegal profession, paralegal education, and salary. The Paralegal Education Program Directory is a searchable database of NFPA-approved schools listed by state.

POLICE

International Association of Chiefs of Police
http://www.theiacp.org

This is one of the oldest police organizations in the country. "Links" contains Web sites of interest to people in law enforcement.

National Sheriffs Association
http://www.sheriffs.org

Explore this Web site for an overview of the field of law enforcement/criminal justice. Select "Membership," then "Career Center" for a look at the type of jobs available in this profession.

SECURITY

American Society for Industrial Security
http://www.asisonline.org

ASIS International is the largest international educational organization for security practitioners. This site contains information on certification, local chapters, and an online forum.

SOCIAL SCIENCES

ANTHROPOLOGY

The American Anthropological Association
http://www.aaanet.org

This organization recently celebrated its 100th-year anniversary. "Jobs/Careers" offers an extensive list of Web-based career-related information, including an article on careers in anthropology. "Links" provides more online resources.

ARCHAEOLOGY

Society for American Archaeology
http://www.saa.org

This site contains information about careers, academic programs, jobs, and opportunities in the field of archaeology.

Archaeological Institute of America
http://www.archaeological.org

The Archaeological Institute of America (AIA) was founded in 1879 and is North America's oldest and largest organization devoted to the world of archaeology. The "Placement Service" provides a glimpse into the type of job opportunities available in this field. "Resources" houses a variety of resources of interest, and "Fieldwork" includes a list of archaeological fieldwork opportunities.

PHILOSOPHY

American Academy of Religion
http://www.aarweb.org

Founded in 1909, the AAR is the world's largest association of academics who research or teach topics related to religion. Visit "Profession" for career and employment information. "Other Resources" provides links to related scholarly organizations.

American Philosophical Society
http://www.amphilsoc.org

Founded in Philadelphia in 1743 by Ben Franklin, this scholarly society promotes useful knowledge in the sciences and humanities.

POLITICAL SCIENCE

American Political Science Association
http://www.apsanet.org

The American Political Science Association is the major professional society for people who study politics, government, and public policies. Read about career options in "Jobs/Careers."

American Academy of Political & Social Science
http://www.aapss.org

Learn about issues of public concern on this Web site.

American Association of Political Consultants
http://www.theaapc.com

The American Association of Political Consultants, founded in 1969, is a bipartisan organization of political professionals. "Links" contains a list of associations, graduate programs, and certification programs.

American League of Lobbyists
http://www.alldc.org

This organization is dedicated to the advancement of the lobbying profession. Visit "Resources" to learn about the art of lobbying.

Association for Public Policy Analysis & Management
http://www.appam.org

Visit "Students" to learn about careers in public policy.

SOCIOLOGY

American Sociological Association
http://www.asanet.org

Visit the "Students" section for information about careers, career preparation, and employment opportunities. There is also a newsletter and a *Guide to Graduate Departments of Sociology*. Great for both prospective and current students.

Rural Sociological Society
http://www.ruralsociology.org

Learn what rural sociologists do at the "Of Interest To Students" section. Appropriate for high school, undergraduate, and graduate students.

Social Psychology Network
http://www.socialpsychology.org

Self-reported as the largest social psychology database on the Internet. Links to more than 5,000 sites related to social and general psychology.

Society of Applied Sociology
http://www.appliedsoc.org

This organization provides a forum for those interested in applying sociological knowledge. Select "Resources," then "Careers" for a helpful article, *35 Things to Think About if You're Considering Sociology*. "Related Sites" contains links to colleges and universities and other sociological organizations.

Sociological Practice Association
http://www.socpractice.org

This is an organization for clinical and applied sociologists. Learn about minimum certification requirements at the masters and doctorate level, ethical standards of practice, and other news about the field of applied sociology.

CHAPTER 15

Math and Science Web Sites

THE MATH AND SCIENCE CAREER CLUSTER

The Math and Science career cluster includes occupations that apply math in research, development, and related activities. People in these occupations generally have interests in *data* and *ideas*. They are creative thinkers that apply mathematical principles to solve problems and research new ideas. Their responsibilities require them to organize, maintain, and evaluate information.

Science occupations deal with research and the application of scientific knowledge to specific problems and situations. People in these occupations generally have interests and skills in *ideas*. They usually have good problem-solving skills, and value inventiveness, accuracy, achievement, and independence. They may be described as curious, logical, precise, analytical, and reserved.

MATHEMATICS

American Mathematical Society
http://www.ams.org

The American Mathematical Society has an extensive Web site that includes a "Careers & Employment" page full of useful information for high school, college, and graduate students.

Association for Women in Mathematics
http://www.awm-math.org

This nonprofit organization's goal is to encourage women in the mathematical sciences.

Biographies of Women in Mathematics
http://www.agnesscott.edu/lriddle/women/women.htm

This site features biographies and photos of famous women mathematicians. Compiled by students in mathematics classes at Agnes Scott College in Atlanta, Georgia, to illustrate the numerous achievements of women in the field of mathematics.

Cool Careers in Math
http://www.coolmath.com/careers.htm

Fun, colorful, interactive site full of games, activities, and lots of other cool stuff for students, parents, and teachers. Appropriate for kids ages 13–100.

Mathematical Association of America
http://www.maa.org

The Mathematical Association of America (MAA) is devoted to the interests of collegiate mathematics. The "Students" section is geared toward college students and contains career and employment resources. If you are interested in teaching math, check out the "Teaching and Learning" section located under "Publications."

Mathematical Sciences Career Information
http://www.ams.org/careers

The purpose of this Web site is to provide mathematics career information in nonacademic areas. Over 90 career profiles of mathematicians working in nonacademic positions. Brought to you by the American Mathematical Society, the Mathematical Association of America, and the Society for Industrial and Applied Mathematics. Funded in part by the Alfred P. Sloan Foundation.

Society for Industrial and Applied Mathematics
http://www.siam.org

Encourages interest in mathematics and in applications of computer science and engineering.

**The Institute for Operations Research and
the Management Sciences
http://www.informs.org**

For a description of what operations research and management science is, select "Education/Students," then "Student Union, "and then finally "Career Center."

SCIENCE

**American Indian Science & Engineering Society
http://www.aises.org**

This national, nonprofit organization bridges science and technology with traditional native values.

**Careers in Science—Women in Research
http://science-education.nih.gov/women/careers**

This site contains biographies of professional women in various science careers.

**Historical Women in Science
http://www.liquidleaf.com/historia/historia.html**

A collection of biographies about famous women in science.

**Science Careers Web
http://www.sciencecareersweb.net**

This site contains valuable information and resources regarding majors in geosciences, marine sciences, biological sciences, and mathematics. Visit "Women in Science" to read career profiles of professional women in science. Published by the Penn State University, Delaware County Campus.

**Society for the Advancement of Chicanos and
Native Americans in Science
http://www.sacnas.org**

The mission of SACNAS is to encourage Chicano/Latino and Native American students to pursue graduate degrees in science professions.

AEROSPACE (SEE ENGINEERING)

ASTRONOMY

American Astronomical Society
http://www.aas.org

The "Career Services" and "Education" sections offer information about careers in astronomy.

BIOLOGY

American Society of Plant Biologists
http://www.aspb.org

Formerly the American Society of Plant Physiologists. Visit "Education" for career-related information.

American Institute of Biological Sciences
http://www.aibs.org

The American Institute of Biological Sciences has been in existence since 1947. The organization is well-established and has a very active public policy branch. To view information specifically about careers in the biological sciences, select "Education Office" under the "Programs & Services" menu.

Botanical Society of America
http://www.botany.org

This organization was established to "promote botany, the field of basic science dealing with the study and inquiry into the form, function, diversity, reproduction, evolution, and uses of plants and their interactions within the biosphere." This site has many interesting features, such as a free spell check feature for botanical spellings, articles, posters, and links to professional journals, as well as interesting botanical links. For career information, BSA has two excellent online publications, *Careers in Botany* and *Botany for the Next Millennium*.

Careers in Biology
http://www.emporia.edu/biosci/carebiol.htm

An extensive list of Web links for information about careers in specific fields of biology. Brought to you by Emporia State University.

BIOMEDICAL (SEE ENGINEERING)

BOTANY (SEE BIOLOGY)

CHEMISTRY

American Chemical Society
http://www.acs.org

The professional organization of chemistry professionals. The "Educators & Students" section offers career-related information and links to other resources.

American Institute of Chemical Engineers
http://www.aiche.org

Web site of the professional organization for chemical engineers. Visit "Careers & Employment" for career-related links for students. "Students & Young Engineers" has information and resources for engineering students.

American Institute of Chemists
http://www.theaic.org

Since 1923, the mission of the American Institute of Chemists has been to foster the advancement of the chemical profession. Also contains a list of links to other professional organizations and resources.

Royal Society of Chemistry
http://www.rsc.org

The Royal Society of Chemistry is the professional organization for chemistry professionals in the United Kingdom. The "Education" section contains a list of publications about chemistry careers that are appropriate for students age 13 and up.

COMPUTER SCIENCE (SEE ALSO COMPUTER ENGINEERING UNDER ENGINEERING; INFORMATION SCIENCES UNDER BUSINESS)

American Association for Artificial Intelligence
http://www.aaai.org

To learn all about artificial intelligence, visit the "AI Topics Website."

Association for Computing Machinery
http://www.acm.org

Select "Students" for information on internships, student membership, and high school programming contests. Read about what employers want from students or browse the ACM student magazine.

Computerworld Magazine
http://www.computerworld.com

Visit "Careers" for an archive of career articles from the editions of *Computerworld* magazine. Articles focus on information technology careers, salary surveys, education, certification, and many other topics.

Girl Geeks: The Source for Women in Computing
http://www.girlgeeks.org

A community and commerce site for women using information technology to advance their careers. Online mentoring, chat, and discussion groups are also available.

IEEE Computer Society
http://computer.org/

Select "Career Services Center" for information about careers in computer science and computer engineering, as well as information on student membership, scholarships, contests, and links to related engineering sites.

Women in Computer Animation
http://www.womeninanimation.org

A professional, nonprofit organization established in 1994 to advance women involved in all aspects of the animation industry.

ECOLOGY (SEE ZOOLOGY)

ENTOMOLOGY (SEE AGRICULTURE)

GENETICS (SEE AGRICULTURE)

GEOLOGY, GEOGRAPHY, & GEOSCIENCE
(SEE AGRICULTURE)

LIMNOLOGY (SEE MARINE BIOLOGY)

MARINE BIOLOGY

American Society of Limnology and Oceanography
http://aslo.org/career.html

Learn how to prepare for careers in the aquatic sciences. This site also offers a "Career Link Program" which contains names and email addresses of former students now employed in the fields of limnology and marine biology.

Careers in Oceanography, Marine Science & Marine Biology
http://scilib.ucsd.edu/sio/guide/career.html

An excellent collection of career information from sources all over the country. This career directory is divided into three sections: oceanography and marine science; marine biology, marine mammals, zoos and aquariums; and general science.

Marine Careers
http://www.marinecareers.net

An excellent source of information about careers in marine science and profiles of people who work in those fields.

Marine Technology Society
http://www.mtsociety.org

Visit "Education" for information on scholarships, careers in the ocean professions, marine schools and centers, and student chapters. Within this section, "Links" includes *"Cool Links for Kids"* which is a list of excellent marine science links for middle and high school aged students.

MEDICINE (SEE HEALTH & HEALTH CARE)

METEOROLOGY

American Meteorological Society
http://www.ametsoc.org

This professional organization promotes education and research in the atmospheric sciences. Learn about membership, events, certification programs, and publications.

MICROBIOLOGY

American Society for Microbiology
http://www.asm.org

Select "Education" for a list of programs and resources for middle, high school, and college students in the microbiological sciences. There are also free career brochures available by request.

American Society for Biochemistry & Molecular Biology
http://www.asbmb.org

This organization offers a free career brochure aimed at high school and undergraduate students who may be considering pursuing careers in biochemistry or molecular biology. Look for their career brochure under "Education."

Society for Molecular Biology and Evolution
http://www.smbe.org

The Society for Molecular Biology and Evolution is an international society for molecular evolutionists.

American Society for Cell Biology
http://www.ascb.org

The American Society for Cell Biology (ASCB) was founded in 1960 to bring the varied facets of cell biology together. "Careers & Opportunities" contains a wealth of career information, as well as a collection of career strategy articles. The Women in Cell Biology committee features their newly published career book, *Career Advice for Life Scientists*. A free copy can be ordered online.

OCEANOGRAPHY (SEE MARINE BIOLOGY)

PHYSICS

Acoustical Society of America
http://asa.aip.org

This organization is concerned with acoustics and its applications. Check out "Listen to Sounds" for excerpts of some interesting man-made, animal, and musical sounds. Career information can be accessed by selecting "Education."

American Institute of Physics
http://www.aip.org

Learn about careers using physics and the latest employment data by selecting "Careers."

The American Physical Society
http://www.aps.org

Visit "Careers & Employment" for career information, employment and internship listings, and a searchable database for graduate programs in physics. The "Education/Women/Minorities" page also includes information on careers in physics, plus resources for women and minority students and professionals.

Institute of Physics
http://www.iop.org

This organization promotes research and education in pure and applied physics. Visit the "Careers" section for career advice, links, and other resources.

STATISTICS

American Statistical Association
http://www.amstat.org

Founded in 1839, the American Statistical Association claims to be the second oldest professional association in the country. The "Career Center" contains a wealth of career and employment information, articles, and brochures for students, women, and minorities. It also features a downloadable *"Career Kit"* that includes an overview of statistics and information on how to become a statistician.

ZOOLOGY

American Zoo and Aquarium Association
http://www.aza.org

This nonprofit organization is dedicated to the advancement of zoos and aquariums in the areas of conservation, education, science, and recreation. Learn about issues, accreditation, and conservation efforts at this Web site.

Animal Diversity Web
http://animaldiversity.ummz.umich.edu

This site is an online database of animal natural history, distribution, classification, and conservation biology from the University of Michigan Museum of Zoology. Includes text, pictures, photographs, videos, and/or recordings of sounds.

The Ecological Society of America
http://www.esa.org

The "Career Opportunities" page has career resources for high school and undergraduate college students. This section explains what ecologists do, the type of jobs that exist, what courses to take, and much more.

National Wildlife Rehabilitators Association
http://www.nwrawildlife.org

This newly-updated site is the home of the National Wildlife Rehabilitators Association. To learn how to prepare for a career in wildlife rehabilitation, visit "Careers." Current news events and scholarship information are also included in this Web site.

National Zoological Park
http://nationalzoo.si.edu

This is the Web site of the Smithsonian National Zoo located in Washington, D.C. To learn about career opportunities, select "Job Seekers" located at the bottom of the page, then "Wildlife Careers." To learn about the 435 different animal species housed at the zoo, select "Animals, etc."

Society for Integrative and Comparative Biology
http://www.sicb.org

For career information about the field of zoology, select "About," then "Careers."

Zoos and Aquariums
http://www.zooweb.com

This fascinating site contains links to zoos and aquariums all over the United States.

References

ACT. *World-of-Work Map*. ACT, 2002. <http://www.act.org/wwm/counselor.html>.

Chickering, A. W., and L. Reisser. *Education and Identity*. 2d ed. San Francisco, CA: Jossey-Bass, 1993.

Dahir, C. A., and C. A. Campbell. *Sharing the Vision: The National Standards*. Alexandria, VA: The American School Counseling Association, 1997.

Department of Counseling and Human Services. "Professional Counselor Portfolio," in *Program Manual*. University of Scranton, 1996.

Division of Undergraduate Studies. *Major Decisions: For Students Who Are Exploring Majors and Other Educational Options*. University Park, PA: The Pennsylvania State University, 1995.

Harris-Bowlsbey, J., Dikel, M. R., & Sampson, J., Jr. (2002). The Internet: A tool for career planning. Columbus, OH: National Career Development Association.

Herring, R. D. *Career Counseling in Schools: Multicultural and Developmental Perspectives*. Alexandria, VA: American Counseling Association, 1998.

Holland, J. L., Powell, A. B., and Fritzsche, B. A. *The Self-Directed Search Professional User's Guide*. Odessa, FL: Psychological Assessment Resources, 1994.

Lancaster, J. L. "About Being an Undeclared Major," in J. N. Gardner and A. J. Jewler (eds.) *College is Only the Beginning: A Student Guide to Higher Education*. Belmont, CA: Wadsworth Publishing Co., 1985.

Lock, R. D. *Taking Charge of Your Career Direction: Career Planning Guidebook, Book I*. Pacific Grove, CA: Brooks/Cole Publishing Company, 1988, 2000.

Moyer, S., K. Witmer, D. Jones, and C. Lauer. "Graduation Projects: Meaningful for the Students, Monitored and Evaluated by the

Staff." Presentation at the Eleventh Annual Conference on Integrated Learning: The School-to-Career Connection, State College, Pennsylvania, November, 2002.

National Association of State Directors of Career Technical Education Consortium. *Career Clusters.* National Association of State Directors of Career Technical Education Consortium, 2002. <http://www.careerclusters.org>.

National Career Development Association. (2001). NCDA guidelines for the use of the Internet for provision of career information and planning services [Statement]. Alexandria, VA: Author. Retrieved from <www.ncda.org/about/polnet.html>.

Northwest Suburban Education to Careers Partnership. *Work-Based Activities: Career Clusters.* Northwest Suburban Education to Careers Partnership, 2002. <http://www.ed2careers.com/work/clusters/>.

Pennsylvania Department of Education. *Pennsylvania Academic Standards for Career Education & Work Standards.* Pennsylvania Department of Education, 2002.

Shahnasarian, M. *Decision Time: A Guide to Career Enhancement.* Psychological Assessment Resources, Inc., 1994.

Sharf, R. S. *Applying Career Development Theory to Counseling.* 2d ed. Boston, MA: Brooks/Cole Publishing Company, 1997.

Tieger, P. D., and B. Barron-Tieger. *Do What You Are: Discover the Perfect Career for You Through the Secrets of Personality Type.* 2d ed. Boston, MA: Little, Brown and Company, 1995.

United States Department of Education. *Career Clusters Homepage.* U.S. Department of Education, 2002. <http://www.ed.gov/offices/OVAE/clusters/>.

United States Department of Labor. *Occupational Outlook Handbook 2000–2001.* Indianapolis, IN: JIST Works, Inc., 2000.

Index